REMEMBERING
RAVENSBRÜCK

HOLOCAUST TO HEALING

NATALIE B. HESS

Copyright © Natalie B. Hess, 2020

ISBN 9789493056244 (ebook)

ISBN 9789493056237 (paperback)

ISBN 9789493056626 (hardback)

Publisher: Amsterdam Publishers

info@amsterdampublishers.com

Frontcover: Natalie with Helena Zylbersztein in Sweden (1947).

CONTENTS

RECOMMENDATIONS

"Natalie Hess' memoir provides an interesting read for a life filled with difficulties and overcoming. Throughout the book you are drawn into Natalie's experiences and it is impossible to put the book down until you are finished. Her journey from child to survivor to immigrant and into adulthood is a story that should be read especially in light of present day. Natalie has a story that is accessible for 8th grade to adults.

I highly recommend reading this book for a glimpse into one person's experience in the Holocaust, but also what a survivor's life is like after, which is often overlooked." - **Shannon Fleischman**, Full Time Educator of Museum and Holocaust Education, Oregon Jewish museum and Center for Holocaust Education

"I finished your manuscript a couple of days ago and immediately went back to read the Holocaust section for the third time.

You have a warm, comfortable style of writing. It seems to beckon the reader to come into your world. There are things about your life the world can never understand. But, there are also many things most can appreciate you verbalizing — awkwardness as a teenager, only two dresses or how to dress, not feeling accepted, feeling there is no place where you belong, etc. These things drew me into "you" and made you a role model who triumphs in the midst of unimaginable circumstances, and yet, walks the same walk as though we were friends and grew up together.

I don't know how long it took you to write this, but the world thanks you for every word and every hour dedicated. It is imperative that no Holocaust hell should be relegated to oblivion." - **Diane McNeil**, Unknown Child Foundation

"Within the vast, ever increasing Holocaust literature Natalie Hess's autobiographical account stands out. Following the chronological sequence of events and eloquently written, often in a dialogue form, it is compelling testimony of a child survivor. At the age of 82, Natalie Hess broke the prevailing code of silence and began to tell her life story.

Intertwining history and memory early childhood images are presented and connected with post-war episodes and reflections. Natalie Hess remembers the horror of the Holocaust – the survival in the Polish ghetto of Piotrow Tribunalski , the cattle train deportation to and the treatment in the women concentration camp of Ravensbrück and the arrival of the "white buses" in April 1945 which brought her and other inmates to Sweden. She spends some years in Sweden, moves to Israel and finally settles down in America.

Reconstructing her long journey she reveals the successful professional career as language teacher and happy family life with a loving caring husband and three adorable daughters, indeed, a child survivor who experienced the Holocaust and succeeded in rebuilding her life." - **Emeritus Professor Dr Konrad Kwiet**, Resident Historian, Sydney Jewish Museum

INTRODUCTION

B'reshit — In the Beginning, or She is Me

Happy Endings
There are no happy endings.
Endings are the saddest part,
so just give me a happy middle
and a very happy start. - Shel Silverstein, *Everything on It,* Harper
Collins, 2011

I am on the 42 bus traveling from Center City Philadelphia to West Philly when, at one of the stops, a bulky, gray-headed lady pushing a walker, struggles up the bus steps. The access is not easy for her. In addition to the walker, she balances two bags and a brown satchel over her shoulder. A red handbag precariously rests on the handlebars of her walker. All the passengers seem to be focused on the spectacle. Is she going to make it?

All of a sudden, three people simultaneously spring into action, a burly middle-aged man and two young women. One of the young women reaches out for the walker. The second tries to give better stability to the sliding handbag. The man offers his arm for support. I feel proud of the young people, and, to tell the truth, I also feel a bit guilty for not being part of the helpful crew. These are good and caring people. For a moment the world is a better place and somehow I am in it.

And then the world isn't.

The burdened lady stands absolutely still on the middle step of the entrance ladder. "You leave me alone!" she shouts. "You sons of bitches, leave me alone. Did I ask for your help? I did not. You stay out of my way. Fuck off. I am doing fine. Just fine. Stay out of my way. Out of my way!"

The helpers, of course, immediately withdraw. A long line has been forming behind the adamant lady. The red light in front of the bus turns green. From behind the bus there are honking sounds. The bus stands still. The driver hums a quiet tune, which clearly proclaims that he is not about to budge until this particular drama has reached its conclusion. The entire collective of the crowded bus holds its shared breath while the lady with great care and interminable resolve, stumbles her way toward the first two seats, which have, of course, been vacated.

As for me? A sense of dishonor in the consciousness of my own hypocrisy floods me. What do I know about this woman and her tragedies? My heart aches for her. At this moment, she is my soul sister. Through her over-the-top behavior she is presenting the act of my own bottled-up emotions. How well I understand her pain, her need for independence, and her craving to reclaim a lost personhood.

Let's call the lady on the bus Rose. Rose who burst apart in her explosive effort to transcend the limitations of her life. I could so easily be her, but I am trying hard not to be. At age 82, when doctors, who could be my grandsons address me by my first name; when in restaurants, the bill is invariably handed to a younger person (the real adult in this show); when during casual meetings, I am treated like so much air as talk is addressed through me to any younger person. And I know that in order to survive, I must learn to be gracious. Yes, I must, but can I? Or must I become Rose?

I have experienced a profound grief and it has caught me in an identity crisis, but I refuse to be stuck in it. There are yearnings on the other side of sadness, and one can be ushered out from inside a shut down world. Who was I? Who am I now? And who do I want to be?

I dedicate this book to the memory of my wonderful husband, my amazing daughters, and my incredible grandchildren.

PART 1
HOLOCAUST

SPIDER WEBS IN MY HEAD

"Verloren gegangen." We are lost.

I heard the German words and I understood what they meant, but the sound of the guttural "monster language" sent icicles down my spine. I felt like throwing up. The back of my throat tasted bitter and I had to swallow hard to keep the bitterness from seeping up into my mouth.

The young couple in front of me were simply lost tourists and they wanted me to give them directions. That was all. I was on my way home from school. I had just gotten off my bike and had dragged it up on the sidewalk. The tires of my bike needed air.

I thought that I had forgotten the harshly arrogant sound of the "monster language." I had certainly tried to forget it. I should have forgotten it by now. After all, it was 1948—three years after I had been rescued from the Ravensbrück[1] Concentration Camp and taken to Sweden by the Swedish Red Cross. It had been a close call.

Helena, our family dentist, and I were among the last to get on those white buses in April of 1945 just weeks before the end of World War II. It was a time when the Nazis were making an effort

3

to get rid of as much evidence as possible, and had we not stepped up on that white bus, we might well have ended as ashes of the Ravensbrück Crematorium.

I was now a Swedish schoolgirl. At least, I was a twelve-year-old girl trying hard to pretend that I was a Swedish schoolgirl. No real Swedish schoolgirl would have become so completely freaked out hearing German. No, but it wasn't just German. I had heard plenty of Jewish refugee German around the house. That German was pronounced with a certain softness, mixed with occasional phrases of Yiddish.

This German frightened me. It had a certain emphasis, a peculiar harshness, a sound that only real Germans made—it was the "monster language" of Ravensbrück.

I made an effort to stop the thoughts that were traveling along the spider webs in my head and I arranged my face in a friendly smile. The German couple looked attentively at me seeming to think me acceptable. I was a girl with a bicycle—not as blond as a real Swedish girl had to be, but evidently they didn't notice. The young woman had her brown hair tied back in a ponytail. She was wearing blue pedal-pusher pants and a puffed-sleeve white blouse. Her smile was open and friendly. I thought she was pretty.

The young man had curly, dark hair. His cap was tipped back. The glasses on his nose slanted forward. He looked puzzled and confused. They were visitors in Göteborg, and they were lost. They were looking for *"Paddan,"* the tourist boat that took visitors through the canals. I knew all about *"Paddan."* I had gone on school trips on the boat. This particular tourist boat also made its journey through a canal right behind the synagogue where the Jews of Göteborg worshipped. I wanted them to know that and I repeated the word "synagogue" several times as I gave them directions.

"Synagogue. Sy-na-gogue." I emphasized the word putting stress on it, making sure that I pronounced it with the heavy German 'Z'sound, and added, *"die Jüdische Kirche"* (the Jewish church) just to make my meaning unmistakable.

I knew that I was being ridiculous. What was I trying to prove? They were just normal tourists in Sweden, not terribly older than me, maybe in their early twenties. They had been children when it was all happening. Perhaps they were among the good Germans. Maybe their parents had been hiding Jews in their basement. What did I know? Did such things really happen, or were these just stories that people told themselves to feel better.

They were nice young normal people. And I was just a Swedish schoolgirl giving them directions. And now they were on their way. End of story!

I had to get home and do my homework, but why had I talked to them in German? I could have just spoken Swedish. I could have pretended that I didn't understand their German. What did they know? People from the monster race. The thing was that they weren't monsters. They were definitely not monsters.

But they were Germans, no denying that! And all Germans were monsters. I knew that! All Germans were monsters— weren't they? The all-powerful monster woman towering above us on her royal platform in Ravensbrück. She had called us to order each morning with her, "*Achtung, Frau Aufseherin.*" That was the woman who could slap Helena across the face. That woman who decided whether we should live or die. She was surely a monster.

But these young people in front of me were clearly not monsters. So how was that possible? But if that was the case, then people, normal ordinary people, had done those dreadful things that they had done. That was a scary thing to think about, very scary because it meant that everyone, all the nice people milling about here on the *Västra Hamngatan* among the department stores, the fancy hotels, and the inviting restaurants, could all do the monster things that the Germans had done.

And what about me? Could I have done those things? Well, if normal people like that nice young couple could do such things, then all people could do such things. Not Helena, of course. No, not Helena. Helena, who had saved my life, could shout and be angry and say nasty things, but she could never do evil.

But other people? Not just Germans? Me too? Everyone except Helena, could we all do evil? Could we all be monsters? I really didn't want to think about it. Not right then. Maybe not ever.

HOW I LEARNED TO BE A LADY

"Why do so many people come to see *tatus* (daddy)?" I ask my mother.

"Your father is the smartest man in town," *mamusia* (mommy) explains. "You are five years old now, so it's time you understood. These are very difficult times, your father is a lawyer, and that means people come to get advice from him." She sighs deeply. "I just hope that he has some useful ideas for his own family."

I know that I am big enough to go to nursery school. I am also old enough to start piano lessons even though my fingers are still not long enough to reach all the black and white keys, but I practice my scales diligently each day—do, re, mi, fa, sol, la, ti do, do, ti la, sol, fa, mi, re, do.

We live in a large apartment on Aleja Trzeciego Maja (The boulevard of the 3rd of May) in Piotrków Trybunalski, Poland. The largest and most important room is tatus's study, because my tatus is a very important man. The parquet wooden floor is always shiny. There is an oriental rug of deep rose and blue and yellow and many colors on the floor. Bookshelves covering the walls are full of important-looking leather-bound volumes, and there is a miniature palm tree in a large, green flowerpot in front of the window next to tatus's big desk. Tatus sometimes lets me hide under his desk, but I have to be very quiet and never bother him.

"Your father is doing important work," mamusia says. "Never disturb him when he works."

I love to hide under tatus's desk. Lucy, too, likes being there. It's our secret house. Lucy is my American doll. Aunt Dora, who lives in America in a place called Evansville, Indiana, sent her to me for my fifth birthday. Today, tatus is talking to a big lady in a fancy fur coat. She leans down and smiles at me, and then she gives me a package, a box full of chocolates, each wrapped in beautiful gold paper.

As fast as I can, I unwrap the first piece, a creamy caramel. It goes past my lips and touches my tongue, and then I taste heaven, a sticky dense sweetness. The chocolate spreads itself over my taste buds. It melts across all my senses and becomes a scrumptious universe of total and completely embracing deliciousness. I finish the entire box, and emerge a smudged, grubby, chocolate addict, not yet knowing that I am marked for life.

Tatus, however, is furious. I have never seen him so angry, and his face scares me. He walks Mrs. Poznanski to the door, and then turns in rage to my mother. "How have you brought up this child?" he thunders. "I am ashamed of her. She is already five years old. She should know better. Have you ever taught her about modesty? About not being such a filthy little monster? About behaving like a lady? My daughter, my daughter must behave herself like a lady. Whatever must Mrs. Poznanski think of us? That was an expensive box of chocolates."

Mamusia is flustered too. She has never received such a box of elegant chocolates.

"You have to learn not to be so selfish," my mother explains. "Before you taste a piece, you must pass the box around to treat everyone else. Only then are you allowed to take a piece, and when you eat it, you do it slowly, just a little bite at a time. That's what a real lady does. You want to be a real lady, don't you? You do want your tatus to be proud of you!"

I look up at the mask of tatus's angry face and I feel both terrified and ashamed. Why did I act so selfishly? What was I thinking? I know that I will never act this way again.

And a few days later, I am tested. Mrs. Poznanski returns, and she brings an even larger box. But this time I know exactly what must be done. Grandma and the cousins are visiting, which gives me a suitable audience. Like a real grown-up lady, I carefully trot about, offering the open box to everyone present, and only later, allow myself the smallest piece, not at all my favorite, but, oh, oh, is it ever worth it! Praise is poured on me. "What an unselfish little girl," the cousins say. "What a well-behaved child," they murmur. "That one will grow up to be a real lady." Tatus too beams with pride, and I feel cushioned and embraced by approval.

Was it then, at the age of five that I realized that such praise was sweeter than the best chocolate wrapped in gold? Was it then that I learned that pleasing others might just become a useful survival strategy? When you are an orphan, pleasing others is a useful skill indeed. Mrs. Poznanski would never know the true value of her tasty gift.

KEEPING A CHILD

I am almost six years old and I like going to play at Jadzia's house. Jadzia lives across the street on Aleja Trzeciego Maja, where my family lived before we had to move to the large ghetto. While the mommies drink tea and talk in the big sunny kitchen, Jadzia and I play with our dolls. Jadzia's tatus is a judge and a good friend of my tatus. I call Jadzia's mamusia, Aunt Fanya, and Jadzia's tatus, Uncle Stephan, even though I know that they really are not related to me and I know that they are not Jewish.

But this time when I am at Jadzia's, things are somehow different. For one thing, mamusia isn't here, and I have been here for many days now and no one has come to pick me up to take me home. I want to go home and I am afraid. Why doesn't someone come? Where is mamusia? Why doesn't Esterke, my babysitter, come to get me? Jadzia is tired of me. She doesn't want to share her toys anymore, and whenever Jadzia and I get into a fight, Aunt Fanya always sticks up for Jadzia.

"When is mamusia coming to get me?" I ask Aunt Fanya. "When is Esterke coming to get me?"

"Your mamusia and tatus had to go away for a while," Aunt

Fanya says, "and you better not mention Esterke again." Aunt Fanya seems angry all the time.

And then somehow, I don't know how, all of a sudden, I know that mamusia and tatus are not going to come back. But I still hope, though I know in my bones that hope is futile. I also know why I shouldn't ever again talk about Esterke, because Esterke is a Jewish name. It is dangerous to have a Jewish name. I badly want to ask more questions, but I know that I better not ask. It is dangerous to ask, it is better not to know.

"Why don't you go home?" Jadzia asks. "Mamusia says that you are my cousin from the country now, but Grandma says that we don't have cousins in the country. Grandma says that we are doing the wrong thing by letting you stay with us. Grandma says that we must get rid of you, and put you in the ghetto. That is the special place where they keep all the Jews."

I know that it is dangerous to be a Jew now, but I also know that the Jews are God's special people. Grandma, who knows everything, has told me all the stories from the Bible and I know that I am Jewish and that Jews have a special contract with God, and that they must never forget that. I try to listen to what Uncle Stephan and Aunt Fanya say to each other after they think that Jadzia and I are asleep and often I hear them whispering the one word. The word is "deported."

"I hear that they have been deported[1]," Aunt Fanya whispers. "They tell me that they could have saved Adek, but he wasn't willing to stay without Reginka. Can you believe that? What about leaving his little daughter? What about that, Stephan?"

"I don't know about that. I don't know anything anymore." Uncle Stephan's voice is not so quiet. "They are counting on us, Fanya, on us, their good friends. My God, what is happening? What are we doing with this child?"

"When can I go home?" I ask.

"I don't know," Aunt Fanya says. "I wish I knew." She sighs and looks scared and worried.

So, then I don't ask any more. I don't want to know, but I know.

When the German soldiers come looking for rooms to rent, I have to hide in the closet where it is hard to breathe, and I have to be very still, because the Germans are looking for Jews and the Jews are all now living in a place called "the small ghetto."

"Mamusia says that you have to be inside the ghetto with all the other Jews," Jadzia tells me. "We can't keep you anymore. Mamusia and tatus say that it's dangerous to keep you here. And I can't tell anybody."

"Why can't they put me in the ghetto?" I ask Jadzia. I don't dare ask Aunt Fanya anymore.

"It's dangerous," Jadzia says. "Nobody knows you are here. Mamusia and tatus can't go near the ghetto."

At night after Jadzia is asleep, and I am supposed to sleep, too, I always listen when Uncle Stephan and Aunt Fanya are talking in the kitchen.

"We can no longer keep the child," Uncle Stephan says. "The neighbors have started to look suspicious. My mother can be a gossip. I am surprised that she hasn't gone down to the courtyard to spread the news yet. And she isn't stupid, Fanya. She doesn't believe a word of your story about the visiting little cousin from the country, and Jadzia has been very good, but she is a child. She won't be able to keep quiet much longer either. Somehow, we have to get this child into the ghetto. I am going to try to get word in. It's either getting her into the ghetto or turning her over, my love. You can see that, Fanya. It's either your family or that little girl. It's good to be good, Fanya, and I love you for that, but it's not good to be stupid. I know what they do to Jew-lovers, Fanya, you know it too."

"Calm down, Stephan. You will wake the children," Aunt Fanya is crying. And then her voice gets angry.

"Why are you blaming me, anyway?" she cries. "You are the one who started all of it. You were the great friend of Adek Chojnacki's. 'He is a great legal mind', you said. 'Who cares if he is a Jew?' Those were your very words, Stephan."

Uncle Stephan bangs the table.

I can tell that he is angry.

"Yes," he says. "I was a fool too. I know, but now we must do something. We must get rid of the child."

"I am going to try getting word into the ghetto," Aunt Fanya is talking through her sobs, and I have to strain to listen. "It's a matter of smuggling in the child, and having someone there sign for her. The Germans keep good records. We all know that. The Zylberstejns were friends of the Chojnacki's. I know they are in the ghetto. Her uncle is running the governing board. Maybe they will be willing to sign for the child. Kuba Zylberstejn works in the glass factory, you know, and he has to pass here with his work party twice a week. If we could just get a message. They are sending Jews out on the trains every day now. Heaven only knows what they do to them."

"For heaven's sake, Fanya. You know very well what they do to them. Let's just hope that they won't do it to us."

"We better think of something to do, my love." Aunt Fanya is weeping again. "She is just a little girl."

INTO THE GHETTO

It is late at night and I am by myself downstairs in the entryway. It's a small dark room. There is a bench on one side of the room and I am sitting on it. I am waiting. I think that I have waited a long time. I need to pee, but I can hold it in. Lucy, my doll, is with me and Lucy is scared, so I hold her tight. "Don't be scared, Lucy," I tell her. "We are going to live in the Ghetto with Aunt Helena and Uncle Kuba. You remember Uncle Kuba, don't you? He is sort of round and doesn't have much hair. Uncle Kuba is married to Aunt Helena. She is a dentist, and she is very beautiful. She has very black hair that she combs into a fancy hairdo on top of her head. She has brown eyes, and a big smile and she laughs a jingly kind of laugh. Remember when she told us that she had to go to Czechoslovakia to learn how to be a dentist, because Jews were not allowed to learn that in Poland? Remember how we had to go downstairs to see her, so that she could pull out that tooth of mine that wouldn't come out by itself? Remember how we were disappointed because she never brought chocolates because she said that chocolate was bad for teeth?"

Lucy doesn't remember so I have to tell her again, and I remind her that mamusia always said that Aunt Helena was a very, very smart lady, and that we should listen to her. And I know that Lucy is worried again. And I have to pee. I hope that Uncle Kuba will come soon, and then I sing a lullaby for Lucy. *"Byly sobie kotki dwa..."* (There once were two kittens).

Singing makes Lucy forget that she is scared, and then I can tell her that Queen Esther is watching out for us, so we don't have to be afraid. I know that I am not supposed to pray to the saints because I am Jewish and Jews don't believe in saints, but Queen Esther is Jewish, too, and she was afraid before she could talk with the king. "So, it is all right to pray to Queen Esther," I tell Lucy.

It is taking Uncle Kuba a long time to come, and now I have to pee very badly. I squeeze tight and wait, but then I can't hold it any longer and a little bit comes out, and then a little bit more and I just can't hold it anymore no matter how hard I try. It comes like a big stream and there is a puddle on the floor and I am cold and wet. I am so very, very much ashamed of myself and I worry that Uncle Kuba will see it. "I couldn't help it," I tell Lucy, and Lucy tells me that it has happened to her too, and maybe Uncle Kuba won't notice.

And then, Uncle Kuba comes. "Hurry," he says, and he doesn't see the puddle. He grabs my hand and pulls me out the door.

I am running as fast as I can to keep up with him. There are a lot of men all around me. Somewhere, there are dogs barking. Lucy is afraid of dogs and she holds onto me tightly. All around me are men's knees and sometimes a knee comes so close that it scratches my face. It is raining, and there is shouting. The knees move on very fast. I am tired and Lucy is afraid. I tell her that we have to move and that there is nothing to be scared of if we just keep going with the knees, and then we are inside the Ghetto.

"Oh, you poor, baby. You are ice-cold." Aunt Helena says, and she is laughing. She hugs and I hug her back. "You have wet your pants," she says, and she laughs.

It is a jingle of a laugh, and I am embarrassed, but I am not afraid anymore, and Lucy is not afraid either. It is a funny feeling not to be scared. I feel like crying, but I remember that tatus told me not to be a crybaby. "People of courage don't cry," he said. "My daughter doesn't cry." So I decide not to cry.

"I am not going to cry!" I tell Lucy, and I don't.

REGISTERED

Aunt Helena shows me how to part my hair neatly. I look in the cracked mirror on the closet door in the bedroom. I struggle to get it right. I am so thin. What has happened to my curls? And my hair has become dull as mouse fir. I remember it being darker. I try to make my face smile, but I don't much like the way it looks.

I know that I have to be registered because otherwise I will be "selected." And I know that being "selected" is very bad. Uncle Kuba and Aunt Helena talk about "register" and "the list" and I know that they are afraid and worried. I know that I am the one that worries them. I know that I am in the way. Sometimes I wish I could disappear. Aunt Helena's father and mother are here too, and they also talk about "register" and "list."

"The child must be registered. - Who is going to register the child? - She has relatives here. Let's talk to them. They will have to register her. After all, she is their flesh and blood. There is going to be a selection again, soon. The child must be registered."

"You must talk to your Uncle Warshawski, Helena. He is, after all, head of the *Judenrat*.[1] He has to help us to get the child on the list."

17

"I did talk to Warshawski. He said I should have talked to him before we agreed to get the girl. He isn't going to help us. He says I got myself into this. You know what he is like."

One day my cousins Rushia and Sabtchia come. They take off their coats and sit on the sofa. They look at me and smile. They drink tea. Rushia puts me on her lap. "Little Nanna," she says. "Sweet little Nanna." Her voice is warm and delicious like melted chocolate, like the sweetness of the orange I had tasted at Grandma Fruma's house, like the *kogelmogel*, the rich egg yolk and sugar mixture that mamusia used to mix for me.

Rushia speaks in the soft melody with a little hiccup in the middle that I remember from before, from long before, from the other life when I still had tatus and mamusia. It is a sweet sound that I had almost forgotten, from before I had to feel scared about things, before I had to be in the way, before I took up too much room. It is all such a long, long time ago. It is like the taste of chicken soup, but that was when there was so much soup, and everyone wanted me to eat, "*Iss, mein Kind*... eat, my child."

But I didn't want to. I was too busy playing. Now, it is a voice from before being hungry all the time, and being too embarrassed to ask for anything. It is the voice of *kogelmogel* and belonging, so long ago.

It all happens fast and then the cousins' voices are gone. The cousins go away.

"They say they would ask their husbands, but I bet we'll never hear from them again," Aunt Helena says. I know that nobody wants me, and wish that I could hide somewhere.

"Someone has to register the child. The child must be registered." The words buzz around me like lost flies.

One day I am in a different house. It's the apartment of Aunt Helena's cousins. It is hot in their rooms and I try to be very quiet and not bother. They are talking in Yiddish, so I won't understand, but I do.

"That Helena is crazy. Think of it... to take on another's child at a time like this... and not ask for advice. Who is going to register the child? She is insane. You know Helena. She has always been that way."

One of the cousins keeps walking up and down the room and talking. She is a tall lady and she walks and talks like she is very angry. "So what if she is a dentist? She may be smart with her books and her hands, but she is dumb like a brick when it comes to people. You know that she will endanger our whole family with this child. Who on earth is going to register this child? The child's own relatives won't do it. Of course not! Who can blame them? It's insane, and Helena is insane. You watch it. We are all going to go because of this child."

And then, Aunt Helena comes to get me.

"I don't want to go to that house again," I tell her.

"Why not?" she asks.

"Because they say bad things about you, so I don't want to go there anymore."

It's the only thing I can think of saying, but I know that I shouldn't have said it. I am scared, and I have a hard time talking without crying. The tears sit back in my throat. I can taste the bitterness. The tears crowd up, and I can't stop them.

At that moment, when I look at Aunt Helena, I suddenly feel that the world is standing still. Something is happening. I stop breathing and I wait. I should say something, but I don't know what.

Aunt Helena stops and kneels down by me. "What did you just say?" she asks, and her voice sounds eerie.

"I don't want to go there ever again."

"And why not, my sweet?"

"Because they said bad things about you. That's why."

Aunt Helena looks at me. Tears gather in her eyes, and she turns away. She takes my hand and squeezes it. "Don't you worry, my sweetheart," she says. "I am going to register you. I don't care what they say. *Que sera, sera. Przyzwalająco.* Whatever will be will be!"

SELECTION

Whispers all around me. "There is going to be a selection." "Yes, it's coming." "Warshawski said it." "Warshawski knows." "There is going to be a selection soon."

Aunt Helena combs my hair carefully and puts a red ribbon on top. "When they come, you sit next to me," she says, "and don't say anything. Just be very quiet, very, very quiet. If we are lucky Schmuel will be the Jewish policeman with them. Your father once did Schmuel's family a big favor. Who knows, maybe Schmuel will decide to pay back."

That very night there is a selection. They go to all apartments in the ghetto. They check the lists and they count all the people. If you are not on their list, then you don't belong. Then they send you away. You are "selected." And I know that you are "selected" to die. That's what it means. I know because Risho, who is my friend and who is two years older than I am, has told me.

"Does it hurt to die?" I ask Risho.

"Not for you," Risho explains. "You are so small and skinny, you will just walk into the gas chamber and die. It won't hurt you one bit. You will just fall asleep and never wake up."

When they come to count, I am sitting on the sofa next to Helena. There are two rooms in the apartment. Helena's parents live in the back room. Helena, Kuba, and I live in the front room. When they come, all of us must be in the front room, so that we can be counted and checked on their list. The ridged cloth of the sofa itches my bottom. I feel bile rising in my throat. I need to pee. My stomach hurts and I want to throw up, but I am very quiet. I bite my lips so that they won't make a sound. They check their list. Everyone has to be on it. Risho's mother says that these are the lists of life and death. She says that they are "the bookkeeping account of mortality." That's what Risho tells me and Risho knows everything.

Aunt Helena is sitting right next to me on the sofa. She is holding my hand. We sit very still but I can feel that she is trembling, and so am I. I feel her hand shaking in mine, and I hear my own teeth knocking at each other, so hard that I think the German must hear them. And if the German hears them, then for sure, I'll be selected.

The German policeman is together with the Jewish policeman. The German policeman is very tall. I think that I remember the Jewish policeman. Was he one of the people who came to talk with tatus? I am not sure. The German policeman just stands at the entrance and watches. He says nothing. He looks at me with his steel-blue German eyes—the monster eyes. He has a gun, but the Jewish policeman has no gun. The Jewish policeman checks the papers. I feel the German looking. I know that he is studying me. His eyes roll all over me. They dig under my skin. They make my skin crawl. The monster eyes feel like big ants crawling up and down—up and down all over me. The monster eyes are sharp knives. They are cutting me to pieces.

I need to cry, but I remember what Aunt Helena told me and I am very quiet. I don't move. I shut my eyes. But even with closed eyes, I still feel the monster eyes on me. I know that they are going to take me away now. I remember that grandma Leeba told me that they always take the children and the old people first, and they had already taken grandma Leeba, so now it was my turn. Was I going to meet Grandma Leeba in heaven like she said? Or, was I just going to go to sleep and never wake up. Just like Risho, who really knows everything, told me?

I feel Aunt Helena's hand squeezing mine, and I feel the trembling between us creeping up from my toes up to the tip of my head, and up to the red ribbon that Aunt Helena had tied in my hair. I really want to cry. I need to cry, but no. I was not going to cry. Tatus had told me not to be a crybaby.

The Jewish policeman looks up from his list. He salutes smartly, and says, *"Alles in Ordnung. Everything here is O.K."* He speaks German, but it doesn't sound the same way as the Germans say it. The German's eyes roll over everyone again. *"Alles in Ordnung,"* he says in the real monster language. And they walk out. The door closes.

Slowly, very slowly Aunt Helena lets go of my hand. We look at each other. The bile in the back of my throat loosens and I cry and cry. And then I see that Aunt Helena is crying, too. She hugs me tight, and I know that I love her. I love her so much, and know that I will always love her. I think that I will love her more than I even loved tatus and mamusia and Grandma Leeba, and more than I love my doll Lucy, and even more than Muchka, my little dog.

I am almost six years old now, and I know that I am so very lucky not to have been selected to die, and I know that life is a treasure, and that I owe it all to Aunt Helena. I know that I will always remember that. Always!

THE BOY WHO NEEDED A PLAYMATE

"They are taking us somewhere else," Risho tells me. "But I don't know where. Maybe this is the place where they'll kill us. Anyway, they are closing this ghetto."

Aunt Helena doesn't know either, but she thinks we will be heading for an *Arbeitslager*. That's a work camp. "Don't you worry," she tells me. "As long as they need someone to reset the jaws of their soldiers who are hurt in the war, they are going to need dentists. I am a very good dentist. We are going to be all right."

"There is a glass factory, Hortensia, nearby. I am sure that they need people to work there," Uncle Kuba says. "They do something for the German war effort."

"As long as they have armies and their soldiers keep breaking their jaws, they will need me," Aunt Helena says. "As long as they need me, we are all safe."

The ghetto is closed and all of us who are left go on buses to Huta Kara Arbeitslager.

There is a tall, yellow fence with wire on top of it all around the Arbeitslager. I stand in a long line before a gate in the fence. A short man stands in front of it. He is wearing a gray suit with a swastika armband on his sleeve. His shoes are black and polished. People with me in the line say that his name is Herr Vogel, and he is the assistant director of the camp. He is checking names on a list, and the people are checked off before they are allowed to walk through the gate.

I am standing in line with Aunt Helena and Uncle Kuba, and with Aunt Helena's parents, Isaac and Guta Sender.

Herr Vogel looks at his list, looks at our group of five people and he shakes his head. "Is the child with you?" he asks.

Nobody says anything.

"Is this child with you?" he repeats, and again there is silence, and I know that nobody wants me. That somehow I shouldn't be there, that somehow I am causing problems.

Herr Vogel looks at me, and I try looking at him, but his eyes won't let me.

"This will never do," he says. "You have two old people and a child. That makes three people who cannot do any useful work. You have to make your choice. It's either the child or the old parents. This is an Arbeitslager, a work camp. I cannot accept three people who cannot do useful work."

And so I know very clearly that I will not be the chosen one. Aunt Helena and Uncle Kuba cannot let their parents go. I realize that and I know that this is the right thing to do, and I know, by now, that I am an orphan and I know that orphans are not wanted by anyone; orphans are in the way. Orphans have to please, and right now, I just don't know how to please, and by now, I also know that not being chosen means that I am going to die. I will be taken away, and put on a train, and taken to a place where they kill people. And I know that not being chosen is because my parents are gone, and understand that I am nobody's first choice. This insults and hurts me more than the thinking about being dead, because I know that once I was loved, and that once I would have been the first choice, the first choice of my parents.

Now I stand at the fence in a space of my own. I am a line of one. I am separated from those who enter.

And then the miracle happens.

Quickly and ever-so-smoothly it happens. Herr Christman, who lives in the big white house above Huta Kara, and who is the boss of Herr Vogel and the director of the camp, comes around the fence, leading a pony. A little boy, Mr. Christman's son, sits on the pony, and the little boy sees the little girl who stands in a space of her own, and the little boy wants a playmate, and so his daddy scoops up the little girl, who rides past Herr Vogel into the work camp. I ride into the Huta Kara Arbeitslager on a pony, and Herr Vogel laughs as he allows the rest of our group to follow.

Did the little boy play with me? Not that I can remember. I don't even know his name, and wherever he lives today, he probably doesn't know that he saved a life at the entrance to the Arbeitslager.

Just one of those coincidences? Perhaps. Who knows? Not I.

JACKET EXCHANGE, TRAIN RIDE, AND ARRIVAL

I am eight years old when the Huta Kara Arbeitslager is dissolved and we are sent on cattle trains to Ravensbrück Concentration Camp in Germany.

Everyone stands outside in an open gathering place. In my memory, the place is wrapped in a brown fog. Uncle Kuba has gone to the men's barracks and I am holding Helena's hand.

There seem to be people everywhere, but there is no sense of togetherness. We are bewildered and confused. Women in uniforms, wearing swastika armbands, are leading large dogs and a loudspeaker barks orders in the monster language: "Women to the right side; men to the left side!"

I cling to Helena. She squeezes my hand and I sense her fear. "Is this the time we are going to die?" I ask.

"I don't think so," Helena answers. "I think that they will still need some of us for the war effort, but I am not sure. It could be. They could be ready to kill us." She smiles and looks down at me. Casual thought of death seems to be the order of the day.

But suddenly Helena's hand tightens in mine. "Oh, my God!" she whispers, and I feel the pulse of her fear growing.

"What is it?"

"The jacket they gave my mother."

"What?"

"Don't you see?"

And now she drops my hand and she is shaking. "It's the jacket they give to all the old people. Don't you see? Don't you understand? They are going to get rid of all the old people right away."

"They are going to kill my mother." The panic in her voice surges. "I've got to do something now! So help me, dear God, I've got to do something!"

Her breath slows down, and then she is thoughtful. She smiles at me. "If they plan to kill the old people now, that means they will still use young people for work. Yes, they still plan on using the young people. So I've got to do something quickly. You wait here," and she rushes across the road to where Guta, her mother, has been placed. She removes her own jacket and exchanges it with that of her mother. She unties the scarf from around her neck and covers Guta's gray hair with it.

She barely finishes, when other older women are removed from the lines, but Guta is ignored, and she now stands in the line of the younger women. Everyone moves to face the Nazi woman in charge of the selection. When our turn comes to meet her, she studies Helena thoughtfully and says something that I don't quite understand, but evidently she has noticed that Helena looks young and assumes that she has been given the wrongly marked jacket. She doesn't seem to see me at all squashed into the line down by those knees.

"That was a tight one," Helena mumbles, but now she is calm again.

There must surely have been stops for relief or for water on the train during those three days to Ravensbrück, but I cannot remember any of that. I only remember that on the train I don't want to take up space. I feel terribly guilty because I don't belong to anybody, because I am an orphan, a person that should not be taking up space. I am sitting on the floor with my knees folded up touching my chin, trying to make myself as small as possible.

I fall asleep sitting like that and I have the same dream over and over again. In my dream on the train to Ravensbrück, I see my tatus's study in our home on Aleja Trzeciego Maja. I see the pine-scented, polished wooden floor, the large window, tatus's wooden desk, and the huge ficus plant on the side of the desk. I can smell the pungent floor polish. The whole scene is at the bottom of a funnel, and as I wake up from my dream it is all sucked up into the conduit and disappears. But it has returned in my dreams—the sharp smell of the polish, the vivid colors of the Persian carpet, the clean touch of the wooden desk, the silky feel of tatus's shoes under the desk where I am hiding, and the sense of utter safety and contentment in a treasured childhood, a childhood wrapped in chocolate.

When we are allowed off the train, there is much shouting. I see barbed wire and search lights and I hear whistles. Huge barking dogs are there, too. Very tall women in black uniforms with many big pockets decorated with even-armed crosses and swastikas, shout directions. Women in striped pajamas and shaved heads are there too. Aunt Helena, Guta, and I are directed to a group of mothers with children.

"You are the lucky ones," a woman in striped pajamas tells us. "You are going to go to a special camp. Your children are going to go to school, and the food will be better."

Helena looks happy, "We are going to a better camp because of you," she tells me and I am happy too. Something good is going to happen because of me. I realize that it has been a long time since I felt this sense of gladness.

One of the women in pajamas stops to look at me. Her shaved head and sharp nose make her look like some kind of predatory bird. She leans over me, and cups my chin in her hand. "Open your mouth," she says, and I do. "Say ahhh..." she orders, and I do. "This child cannot travel," she shouts. "This child has to be kept in the barracks for the sick. She has scarlet fever. Whoever is with this child has to stay!"

Aunt Helena, Guta, and I are all moved away from the line of those who are going to continue the journey to that special camp. Helena looks down. She is sad and disappointed. An avalanche of guilt washes over me. I have failed again. They have to stay because of me. Everything is my fault.

Not until after liberation, do I learn that all of these mothers and children were shipped to Bergen-Belsen, where most of them died of disease and starvation. The woman in prison pajamas, who had looked in my mouth, was a Jewish prisoner, a physician, who somehow knew I was an orphan and had evidently decided to save the life of one little girl. I never had scarlet fever.

LICE

I stand in line behind Helena when we first arrive in Ravensbrück. Everyone has their hair examined for lice, and if lice are found, heads are shaved. Female prisoners in pajamas do the examining. Hair lands on the floor in big chunks that look like dead animals. Beautiful women change into skeletal shades of their former selves. Female shapes grow strangely bird-like and warped. Faces look wasted. Eyes grow large and distrustful. Female softness is erased and facial expressions grow sternly fearful.

Inside of me fear grows. I can't stop trembling. Somehow even though I am just eight years old, I know that what I see is a process of degradation, an obliteration of spirit. Each woman is losing a core piece of self. I am waiting in fear, but I know exactly what is going to happen to me.

Ten women are ahead of Helena and me in line. Each one of them succumbs to the shaver and emerges in the diminished crow-like form. When Helena's turn comes she is examined and, as my inner vision had predicted, her head is not shaved. Helena does not have lice. Lice are great equalizers. Everyone in Ravensbrück has lice. Everyone except Helena. Helena is up every morning before

31

5am. She washes her hair and scrubs her scalp with ice-cold water every single morning. She manages this feat even in Ravensbrück, where the roll call is at 5am. In my memory, Helena's head will be the only unshaven one to leave Ravensbrück in 1945.

I stand right behind Helena in line, and I know that right now they are not going to find any lice on me, either. Throughout our lives at Huta Kara, Helena has included me in her regimen, but I also know that here at Ravensbrück, she will not be able to do that, and I am going to get lice. I know for sure that I will.

Here right now they are shaving everyone's head, and I desperately want to be just like everyone else. More than anything, I need to be like everyone else. More than anything else, I want to be like everyone else, but it is not going to happen.

The beautiful Ilana, a girl whom I so much admire, and whose thick coal-black hair is beautifully braided, bends to the shaver as her hair falls to the ground and she joins the denuded female crowd. I know that I will be excluded, only to be caught later. And I will have to be shaved publicly and alone, and everyone will know that I have become a dirty one. Doing it with everyone makes it a regular thing, an ordinary thing, and the ordinary is never shameful, but I will stand out and be publicly known as scum.

I know that later when it happens, Ilana, especially will notice and she'll humiliate me and mock me and I dread the coming mortification.

And indeed, my predictive script is fulfilled. At first, I am allowed to keep my curls, but lice are found during a later inspection, and indeed my hair is shaved in front of everyone.

I don't know why I cry so long and so hard during the procedure. After all, I knew it was coming, but I simply cannot stop the sorrow. I am eight years old and I am a girl, but somehow I feel that it is my long hair that made me a girl and that with its loss my sense of self has been diminished and demolished. My girlhood has been stolen. I am overwhelmed with sadness. I cry and cry even though no one hears me and there is no response. I cry for the girl who was me—the girl who is no longer there.

"You filthy one!" Ilana taunts, just like I knew she would, but at least I am not surprised. "When we first came, they shaved everyone," Ilana scornfully points out, "but now they had to take you special. That means that you really are the dirty one. You got lice for sure! The rest of us were just part of the routine. You are pathetic! You are an orphan! You are grubby!"

I have nothing to say. Intuitively, I know that the best thing I can do is to be quiet. But back on the rough pine shelf-bed covered with a thin straw mattress, that has become our home[1], I cry and cry. It seems that I will cry over my lost hair and my lost girlhood forever.

HUNGER

Hunger was a constant companion in Ravensbrück. It was the expected and unvarying presence. It was like an accompanying and unnerving ogre that steadily gnawed. It was an ubiquitous empty cavern–the sucking fiend that could not and would not be satisfied. One small chunk of dark bread every day was the ration, and much as I wanted to save it like Risho was able to do, I never could. When the precious bread appeared, I would first break of a tiny crumb and rest it on my tongue like a blessing that soon evolved into an unbearable itch, and then scratch like a tyrant. "More, more, please, I want more," my tongue screamed, and I could never deny it. In a split second, the entire piece disappeared leaving a dull pain and a desperate longing for more.

Some days the echo of pain faded but on other days it would become a wailing and pleading orchestra that pierced at me with a harassing cry.

Bread was the currency of the camp. For two slices one could buy half a cup of milk. Mostly, the milk had been diluted with water. Once, the Red Cross brought milk for the children and I drank mine in a stupor of foaming ecstasy. Risho, who was my friend from Huta Kara, watered his portion of milk, and somehow managed to sell it for three slices of bread. I never knew where and how he conducted these business affairs.

"That one is going to be a great businessman when all this is over," my new friend, Anna-Lise said. Anna-Lise was grown up at nineteen, yet she treated me like an equal. She had become a sort-of friend, even though I knew that she was German, so I never completely trusted her. She wore a black triangle on the sleeve of her prison pajama, instead of the reversed red one with the letter 'P' on it on top of the yellow triangle that I wore and that marked me as a Polish Jew.

"Don't you know what black stands for, you little dope," Risho taunted.

But I didn't really mind his constant insults.

He was, after all, two years older than I, and he was the first one who had told me that they were killing people in gas ovens.

"It's nothing you need to worry about," he had explained. "You are so small and skinny, you will die right away."

"What happens when you die?" I asked.

"Nothing," he explained. "You just go to sleep."

Another time, he had taken down his pants to show me how boys are different from girls. It looked out of place and uncomfortable, and I was glad to be a girl.

Risho also knew everything about the patches that spelled out our identities in Ravensbrück. "Black means that she is a German prostitute. So, she is a real criminal—not like us who are here just because we are Jews. Be careful of her. She is a German criminal. Who knows what she can do?"

I had no idea what "a prostitute" was, but Risho knew the world, so he was probably right. But I did like Anna-Lise and I thought she was very pretty with her large blue eyes and the bits of blond hair that were growing out.

One day there were packages from the Swedish Red Cross, and there was candy for the children. I got a glossy, ruby red one in the shape of a raspberry, and I thought that it was the most beautiful thing I had ever seen. It clung to my palm with delectable stickiness, and I wanted it both in my hand and in my mouth. A sense of reverence filled me as I put it on my tongue and slowly sucked it, scarlet spreading over my taste buds. The sweet, totally satisfying tang spread through my body wrapping me in a blanket of syrupy gratification, and my tongue danced around it.

Then suddenly, without warning, it was gone, but the taste still lingered. This too vanished and I bit my lips trying to recapture it, and then I cried bitterly over its desertion. The tears brought an acid taste to the back of my throat, killing the last vestiges of sweetness. Nothing has ever replaced it.

To this day I don't understand why the Red Cross packages were delivered to people who had been scheduled to die. The logic of the system continues to defy me, but then logic doesn't operate in the structure of casually accepted evil.

SWEDISH BUSES

Spring 1945. We are herded into a barrack outside of the official premises of the camp. We are squashed together in much the same way as we had been on the trains when we first arrived to Ravensbrück.

A woman next to me is whimpering, "I don't want to die. I don't want to die. Please don't let me die."

I hear what she is saying, but somehow it doesn't touch me. I feel too numb to care. "Are we going to die now?" I ask Helena.

"Maybe," she mutters.

A leaden weariness envelops me. I should care, I really should be afraid, but I don't feel anything except this foggy sense of total indifference and lethargy.

There has been no food for three days, but I am no longer hungry. Sometimes I sleep, and sometimes I am awake, and then once a vibrant dream visits me.

In the dream, I am walking on Aleja Trzeciego Maja in Piotrków. I am walking between tatus and mamusia, and I am holding their hands. One parent on each side. I am the one who is holding them together. I am essential. I am their link of love. A stream of devotion and safety flows from those two parental hands —one on each side—into mine. As we walk, I hold their hands tighter, and I am filled with an overwhelming joy, a sense of wellbeing and of shelter, a sense of belonging. I am in the right place. I am where I belong.

As we walk in the dream, I begin to skip, and the parents seem to be humming. *Mamusia is beautiful*, I tell myself in the dream. She is the most beautiful woman in the whole world. I glance at her, and I feel the motion of her stride. The silk of her flowered summer dress sweeps against my hand. I recognize it as her Shabbat dress. I look down on her feet, and I see her glistening glass slippers like the ones I always imagined Cinderella must have worn. On my other side, tatus's somber black, shiny shoes move with a steady rhythm. I lift my head as we walk, and I feel protected, and I am proud, and the spring wind touches my cheeks and blows through my black hair.

When I wake up, I still feel snuggly ensconced in the dream. And suddenly I also know two things. I know for sure that I am not going to die, and I also know that I will never see my parents again. Neither one of these two realizations seems surprising. That is just the way it is.

On the morning of the third day in the new barrack, the doors open and three German women monsters appear. They have their great dogs with them, but they are not dressed in uniforms. They are wearing quite ordinary women's clothing, and look more mundane—sort of, like normal women, a bit on the dowdy side. One is wearing a green dress. The other two wear brown skirts and white blouses, but everything looks wrinkled and shabby, even as they shout their orders. They make us line up in rows of four. They walk between the rows tearing off our prisoner insignias from our sleeves.

I look around with wonder and notice things I hadn't seen before. We are standing outside of the camp, and it is beautiful here. The natural beauty of the place astonishes me. There is a lake framed by birch trees. There is rustle of leaves and the sounds of early bird song and the smell of morning newness.

"Was this always here?" I ask Helena. "Was all this out here when we were in there?"

Helena squeezes my hand. "Now they will either kill us or set us free," she says. "I don't care."

Then, from somewhere there is a loud voice in German. "The Swedish buses are here!" the voice announces. "Run, the Swedish buses are here! Run!"

We are all running. I feel my legs folding under me, but I get up and continue to run, and there are those huge, white buses—the buses to Sweden, the buses to salvation.

Forty years later, a survivor whom I meet in California, tells me that the Nazis had put poison in the bread rations to get rid of as much evidence as possible in these waning days of the war. The Jewish prisoners who served as bakers for the camp discovered the change in recipe and buried all the bread.

In the 1970s, the Swedish white buses arrive in Jerusalem to serve as memorials at *Yadv'shem*, Jerusalem's Holocaust museum.

I travel from Jerusalem, where I then live, to Haifa, so that I can see the arrival of those "huge buses." They really are quite small—each about the size of a small American pickup truck, but in my memory they will always be those huge buses of saving grace.

SO, WHAT IS IT ALL ABOUT?

I always thought that I would go back to Poland someday, but it was *someday*, yes, *some day*—that eternal and everlasting *someday*. Well, I would really do it *someday*, wouldn't I? And I usually keep my promises; even those that I make to myself. So that was the plan. I was going to do it *someday*. And then, suddenly, just like that, *someday* arrived. Of course, it came via an invitation in my email inbox. What else would you expect?

A trip was being organized from Israel by a fellow called Natanel Yechielli. It would be a special tour for Piotrków Trybunalski survivors and their descendants. Natanel Yechielli himself was one of these. People were evidently signing up from all over the world—there might be participants from Canada, from Australia, from Great Britain, from the US and, of course, from Israel. Was I interested? What a question! After all, I had been planning to do it *someday,* hadn't I? Well, lady you are 81 years old. How many *somedays* do you think you have left?

Yes, I know. You don't need to remind me. But do I really want to go there? Is there really a Poland out there on the map? Is there really a Piotrków Trybunalski?

I have spent 75 years thinking of a Europe without these places. For so long, Piotrków has just been a floater outside my vision of reality. Yes, yes, don't tell me. I know what the geography of Europe looks like, but Poland is still not a real place where people pick up their mail, eat ice cream, laugh at stupid jokes, a place without Jews, a place that once was one third Jewish, but where not a single Jew now lives, a place where the beautiful synagogue has been turned into the city library, but where one wall in that library is still full of the bullet holes marking the places where Jews, including my grandmother, were lined up and shot.

Of course, I register for the trip. I buy a new suitcase, and I get my ticket at the AAA on the corner of Market and 20th, where the agent doesn't bat a single long eyelash at the notion that I am heading for Piotrków Trybunalski. And then, much to my delight, two daughters, a son-in-law and a granddaughter decide to join me.

To tell you the truth, I am a bit frightened by the whole thing. Why do I want to go there, anyway? Here at the edge of the end of life, why do I suddenly feel the need to go? Am I hoping to learn something new and relevant for the rest of my life? Is there something of myself that I feel must be excavated—something that I left behind? Am I trying to put a ribbon on the package of my life?

A Canadian airplane takes me to Toronto where it gives me a five-hour break for coffee, plus all sorts of delightful junk food, which I happily allow myself to indulge in. Heck, I can worry about reasonable eating when I get back home. Now I am away from the real world, so I might as well go whole hog.

I love traveling by airplane because it puts one so completely in another's hands. When you drive, you must constantly worry about being in the right lane, making the right turn, invariably consider all those crazy drivers with whom the road must be shared. Even in today's world of Mrs. GPS with her modulated voice, there is plenty to fret about, if nothing else, you can always disagree with the voice, and do your own thing. Even when you travel by bus or by train, there is plenty to be concerned about. Did you catch the right one? You better not miss the place where you have to get off.

None of this occurs when you fly. The airline will call you when they want you, and all you have to do is follow their often repeated and clear instructions. Turn off your cell. Turn off your anxieties. These winged ones are here to worry for you. Of course, they can always crash, but that's not your problem. Is it now? No, when going by air, you can turn your control buttons off. This is one place where you are not in charge of your own destiny, sister—and ain't that a relief?

Our first stop is, of course, Warsaw—Warszawa—the dream city rebuilt brick by brick in 1945. Today it is a booming modern European place, and naturally, we begin with the Museum of Jewish History in Poland. They give us 45 minutes to cover the core exhibition, which is about like giving a kid his favorite box of chocolates, provided he can eat all of it in three minutes.

At any rate, the basic story is this: Jews doing well under some Polish kings and very badly under others. This is the story told through art, literature, music and extraordinarily clever, interactive techno-dramas.

The kings have names like Boleslaw, Dytryk, and Casmir. The word Poland itself seems to have come from the Hebrew words *Po* and *Lyn,* meaning, "here we rest," which the Jews did for about one thousand years. But actually it wasn't the greatest rest, and it definitely ended, if not in 1945 then surely after the communists took power in 1968. The spectacular place sends out huge beams of irony. All this glory, without Jews in Poland. What a wonderful story—not the slightest hint of its hellishly dark conclusion. I sense an aura of Disneyland. Real this is not!

We leave the museum and move into the Jewish world of Warsaw as it exists today. I sense a different dimension of historicity and reality as we enter the Nozyk synagogue, the only synagogue that survived WWII, as Rabbi Blum now tells us.

Rabbi Blum is a clean-shaven young man, dressed in dark

trousers and a white open-necked shirt. He is the assistant rabbi of Warsaw and he finds the position challenging. He addresses us in Hebrew. We are a multilingual group and everything gets translated into three languages: Polish, Hebrew, and English. Natanel, our Israeli leader, has turned into a superb linguist as well as a competent translator.

"How many Jews actually live in Warsaw now?" a Canadian from our group asks.

Rabbi Blum hesitates and adjusts the crocheted *kipa*, which is rather precariously moving about on his curly black hair. "I am not sure exactly how many there are just now, but the last I heard, there are close to five hundred."

"How many Jews lived in Warsaw before the war?" someone up front wonders.

"I am not sure. That is, I don't have the exact number, but I do know that there were about 600 synagogues in Warsaw before the war, and they were all destroyed."

"And how did this one survive?" a female voice somewhere in back asks.

Rabbi Blum pulls a white handkerchief from his pocket and wipes his face. Again, he lifts his *kipa*, in a nervous gesture, pats it down, and adjusts the small clip that keeps it fastened to his dark hair. "Good question," he says. "It survived because the Nazis used it as a stable, and a storehouse for the food of the horses. As you know, one of the ways in which the Nazis showed their derision for the Jews was to destroy anything connected to Jewish culture, so it is indeed quite miraculous that this particular building did remain. And now, there are services here every Shabbat. Also, another interesting phenomenon seems to be taking place, and frankly, I don't know how to handle it, yet."

Rabbi Blum pauses. A small smile lights up his features. He suddenly seems very young. "The miracle of the Jewish daughters," he murmurs. "It's a long story. Let's see, where shall I start?"

"At the beginning," someone suggests.

"Ah, yes," says the rabbi. "The beginning... First of all, you should understand that it's cool, yes very cool, like you Americans say, to be Jewish in Poland today. There are really so very few Jews around. And then, Jews do stand for cosmopolitanism, and, of course, being cosmopolitan was an absolute sin during Communism, but now that Communism is gone, what all good Poles heartedly desire is to be part of the West, so being Cosmopolitan is a very good thing—a great thing. And Jews, of course, are a symbol of all this. Jews, like you, come from the West. You speak English—the new world language. You buy stuff, you travel, and yes, you are clearly Westerners."

It is not a bad thing, the dark secret that Grandma whispers to her beloved granddaughter.

"I want to tell you something," Grandma whispers. "I am a Jew. Nobody knows, but I am a Jew, and because being Jewish depends on who your mother is, and that means your mother, whether she knows it or not, is also Jewish, and that means, of course that you, too, are Jewish. You are Jewish, my beloved granddaughter, and I want you to know that. Do with it what you want, my dear, but this is my legacy to you."

So that's why the granddaughters come to me. 'You are the Rabbi,' they tell me. 'Now what do I do with that?' they ask. What is it all about?'"

"Wow!" Someone in our group exclaims

"Yes," says the rabbi, "Wow is about it. But in a way, it is also a story of its own time. This is the Polish story right now."

"So what do you tell them? How do you deal with this?"

"Truth is," Rabbi Blum muses, "I haven't decided how to handle it."

"How did they survive the war?" a woman from the US asks.

"Some, of course, survived on false papers, but 20,000 returned to Poland after the camps were liberated in 1945."

"After everything that had happened, how could they return to Poland?" someone wonders.

"Well, it must have seemed like the natural thing to do," Rabbi Blum explains. "Poland, after all, had been a Jewish home for almost one thousand years. But you have to understand that anti-Semitism was running high. The returning Jews were definitely not welcome. The slogan then and well into 1968 was: *Poland for Poles, and Palestine for Jews.* By 1968 most of the Jews had left. Those who remained probably had made the decision that they no longer wanted to be Jewish."

As I listen to Rabbi Blum, I try to remember where I had been in 1968. Yes, of course, of course, why hadn't I thought about it before? In 1968, I was a teacher of English at the Hebrew Gymnasia in Jerusalem, and like the rest of the faculty, I had been somewhat surprised at the influx of new students from Poland that year. Now it is 48 years later, and what does one tell this young woman, who suddenly discovers that she is Jewish and comes to ask the rabbi what this is all about?

I don't know what on earth the rabbi will tell her, but I have been mulling the thing over as I think through the possibilities.

"You have made a very interesting discovery, my friend," I might tell her, "and here are some possibilities for you: You can just forget the whole thing. Grandma was dying. She had not lived as a Jew and there is no reason for you to do so, either. Her legacy, no matter what she said was her life, not her death. She had made her choices and you are entitled to make yours. But, of course, there are other ways of considering what you have just learned. In my view, destiny has given you a unique chance in life's lottery. You can, if you so wish, join up with a remarkable civilization that began about five thousand years ago. You can, if you so desire, take a look at a very old, persistent, and vibrant book discussion group that seems to go on without an end. The book is, of course, the Hebrew bible. It's full of good stories and also lots of rules. Lots of do's and lots of don'ts. You can decide to be part of the first bunch who got the book, and said that they would try it out. You should know that those first Jews who received the law weren't all that enthusiastic about it. They responded with, 'Okay, we will do and we will listen.' (*nasev'nishma*), which is kind of peculiar. You might have expected them to listen first and do later, but they are not the greatest listeners. They just started doing, so that's what you might do. Pick something that appeals to you from the book and just do it. Maybe light candles on Friday night. That's in the "do" column and that would have been my choice. If you want something from the "don't" column, you can always give up pork, that, for some reason, seems to be a popular choice, but there are actually 613 possibilities. All I know is that doing or not doing comes first. That is before any spiritual uplift. Ritual before revelation seems to be the way this thing works. You might want to check it out. Who knows, it might even work in today's Poland."

And then, of course, there is dear Rabbi Hillel, who was asked by, I believe, a Greek, to explain all of Judaism during the time the asker was able to stand on one foot. Rabbi Hillel did not hesitate. "Don't do to others what you don't want them to do to you," he said. "All the rest is commentary. Go and study it!"

It's a bit on the vague side. I personally like things to be more concrete, but the important thing is to get started—do one thing. It's like riding a sleigh. It's that first little push at the edge of a hill and then it goes, and you never know where it might take you.

Right now it is the rabbi's story that has taken me into the embrace of Jewish Poland as it is today. I could have been one of those grandmothers, had I returned to my hometown, Piotrków, in 1945.

Instead, I wound up in Sweden, later in the US, and still later in Israel. I have always recognized my Jewish heritage as my enriching essence. I have raised three Jewish daughters, and they, in turn, are bringing up my six Jewish grandchildren. But I understand that I could so easily have become one of the whispering grandmothers, if fate had dictated a return to Poland for me. I would like to talk some more with Rabbi Blum, but the bus for

Piotrków is waiting, and I am just an American tourist, perhaps one in search for a recognizable identity card, lost somewhere in Poland around 1943.

HOLDING TIME

Everything happened yesterday. Yesterday, I was a loved child. Yesterday, I became an orphan. Yesterday, I was starved, and my head was shaven. Yesterday, I was a schoolgirl in Sweden and an immigrant to America. Yesterday, I was a young bride and a young mother. Yesterday, I met John. Yesterday, I was a teacher, and I taught teachers. Yesterday, I lived and worked in Jerusalem. Yesterday, I became a grandmother. Yesterday, I also became a widow, moved to Philadelphia, and started to recreate my life as a single senior woman.

Very seldom does a yesterday join today. Yet there are those moments, and they are irreplaceable. At these unique times, a particular light shines and all the yesterdays hook up with today.

Seventy-three years ago, I left Piotrków Trybunalski as a half-starved orphan on my way to communal slaughter. I come back today supported by two daughters, one granddaughter, and a son-in-law. I come back with an American passport in my purse and dollars in my pocket, but I walk the town as a ghost. It is my son-in-law, Ronen, who first notices the ghostly quality of our presence.

We are a group of 30 people. Only four of us are actual

survivors, Charles from New Jersey, Gershon from Israel, Michael from England, and me. The rest are what we call "second or third genners," children and grandchildren, the miracle babies who were never meant to be born—just as the four of us who were never meant to continue our lives. We walk, talk, and eat ice cream in a pleasant little restaurant on Reynek Trybunalski, the main town square. We search and we find addresses where our families once lived and we take pictures of the indentations made by our Mezuzot[1] still left on their doorposts.

There is constant buzz of recollection. "This is where my uncle lived. - This is the road I went to school. - That's my grandmother's store. - My grandfather was the kosher butcher. - That was the street that marked the beginning of the large ghetto."

But as we walk and talk there is, as Ronen points out to us, a curious sense of our own invisibility. The locals seem to know exactly who we are, but no one looks at us. There is no eye contact.

There is a definite sense of our absence in our very presence. We are the spirits who have returned, and we will surely go away soon. Nothing is said. Don't look; don't ask; don't interfere. They are here for a reason. If they ask anything, please do answer! Do be polite, but don't stare. Don't offer help. They come and go. This bunch, like the one before it and the one before that, will go away, too! Nothing happened here. Absolutely nothing.

We note that a great part of the town has been rebuilt and reconstructed. The restaurants and coffee shops around Reynek Trybunalski have a Disneyland feeling—all is colorful awnings and beautifully arranged flowers containers—mostly in red and white, the Polish colors.

The town square is bathed in sunshine. There are lots of Polish flags. The parish church looms above all. There is an abundance of churches in Piotrków. I look into only one, but there are at least four more, so that walking about the town one always feels in the shade of a church.

The Sanctuary of Our Lady of Piotrków dates back to 1640. I

am somewhat amused by the date as I know that this particular year marked the first arrival of Jews in America. No connection at all, but these things do bounce around in my mind.

There is also a large part of town that has not been restored. Bombed out and boarded-up houses stay as they were in 1945. Those parts of town seem to be in a state of traumatic blackout—a strange unconsciousness. Sleeping beauty waiting for that kiss of the prince. Well, we are not going to be that prince. That's for sure.

At Aleja Trzecejgo Maja number 4, we walk up the stairs to my family's first apartment home in Piotrków. It has been turned into an office of sorts. People are busy at their computers. We are allowed to walk through the offices and no one bothers us. We are the ghosts. Occasionally, one of the office workers tosses us a furtive look, but when we try to make eye contact, they look away. *Whatever you do, don't look at the ghosts. If you just ignore them, if you just don't pay attention to them, they will go away. They were never here.*

We walk through the apartment, that has been turned into an office and I try to locate our life there. Voices come up from the stairway.

"Number 4 is the place where the lawyer, Chojnacki, lived with his family," I hear the voice of Gershon Klein, explaining to a small group that follows him. I remember that Gershon and his wife, Pnina, had been sitting right behind my daughter and me on the bus to Piotrków and we had briefly chatted. "My family lived right up the street on number 9," Gershon's voice now continues.

"Lawyer Chojnacki was my father," I interrupt. And then suddenly all is quiet. Somehow the silence spreads and then time stops.

Gershon stands still and looks at me. "You are Nanna Chojnacka?" he says with incredulity in his voice. His face is wrapped in wonder. "I know you from the time you were a baby. I was four years old when you were born." A slow smile spreads across his face. "It's kind of embarrassing to tell you this," he says.

"But I saw you naked in your first bath. Our mothers were best friends since high school. Don't you remember me?"

"Oh my God! You are Genek?" I ask, and time floats in on an encompassing wave. "You were the tall boy who was terribly bored with me. The boy that I admired so much. It was really you."

"The same," he says, and we hug.

For a moment, all days are one, and all the yesterdays hang together in a glorious chain of order and possibility. We would probably never see each other again.

PART 2
LIFE IN SWEDEN

SWEDEN, THE NATIONAL ANTHEMS OF MY LIFE

We are a group of women and children who have recently been liberated from the Ravensbrück Concentration Camp in East Germany and brought to Sweden in the white buses of Count Folke Bernadotte.[1] Our heads are shaved and our emaciated bodies have little to cover our skeletal forms. I am nine years old and the only child in this particular group.

We are temporarily housed in a school that has been closed for summer vacation, but on this afternoon, we are guests for coffee at a Lutheran parsonage. The parsonage drawing room is the most beautiful place I have ever seen. Its essence of comfort and contentment will remain a pattern for all the homes I will create one day for my husband John and me during our 53-year marriage.

The room we enter is bathed in blue-gray Swedish summer twilight. White curtains billow at the windows, brushing the red geraniums on the windowsills. Hand-woven throw rugs accentuate polished blond wooden floors. Family portraits line one wall, contented ancestors giving us a benevolent nod. Books are neatly stacked on shelves that cover the whole of another wall. A crystal bowl of fruit glitters amidst family pictures on the baby-grand piano. I notice the soft scent of a lilac drifting inward from the garden.

Seven varieties of iced petit fours, as demanded by Swedish custom, entice us. Remembering the lesson taught me by my father in that other life I once lived, where I had been so strictly reprimanded for grabbing forbidden chocolate, I keep my fingers away from the fancy small cakes, even though I desperately want one.

We have clearly journeyed from hell to heaven, and we know it. Some of us must surely feel the anxiety of knowing how temporary this state will be, but most of us, certainly including the little girl who was me, are joyously absorbing this helium of happiness and making a spiritual flight upward into a blissful regeneration of the moment.

Elsa, the parson's wife, appealingly round, circulates offering us delicious homemade fare. She smiles and chats with each of us, speaking a perfect German personalized by her lilting Swedish. As she moves, her loosely shaped yellow dress flows around her, showcasing her upswept blond hair. I can't take my eyes off her. She is the good and beautiful fairy from stories. She is Queen Esther from Purim[2] translated into Swedish blond.

One of the older, maternal women turns to our hostess and asks, "*Liebling*, why don't you eat some of these wonderful things?"

Our hostess blushes, and much to our amusement answers, "Oh, I am too fat. I must diet and lose some weight."

Her response is greeted by a huge lighthearted peal of laughter. We are all in such a state of harmony that disparagement of any kind is utterly out of place. To our skeletal selves, Elsa is the perfection of beauty.

Skinny is ugly. Fat is beautiful—the fatter, the better—isn't that obvious?

"*Du bist eine Schönheit... du bist eine Schönheit,*" (You are a beauty) we warble in unison.

Even I, the totally uninformed child that I am, clearly

understand the essence of pulchritude. One has to have flesh on the bones—the more the better. The bride price is higher for a woman of weight. A pretty woman has to be *"saftig"* (juicy), rounded out—good to squeeze. Everyone knows that!

One of the women sitting close to me mutters an old Polish adage, "By the time the fat man gets thin, the thin man will be dead."

Those who hear, nod in agreement, but it is all giddy banter. We are, after all, guests at a wonderful party and the atmosphere is peacefully exultant.

We sit together in nationality groupings: Poles, Czechs, Hungarians, and Lithuanians. I believe that all of us are Jewish. Our common language is German, which we picked up in the camps.

Our host, the parson, infuses the room with male presence. Tall, thin, dark-haired man, his clerical collar seems to choke him. He sits at the baby-grand piano and plays the Swedish National Anthem.

He and his wife sing it together, *"Du gamla, Du fria, Du fjällhöga nord, Du tysta, Du glädjerika sköna..."* (You ancient, you free, you mountain high north, you silent and joy filled beauty.)

It is the first time I hear the song, which will later become such an integral part of my schooling and the foundation of what will become my Swedish identity.

The pastor encourages, or perhaps even commands, each group to stand up and sing our national anthems.

"Your turn, ladies!" he insists. "All of you have national anthems. Now let's hear you sing with pride! Stand up and sing. I want more national anthems. Show your national pride, ladies."

A collective embarrassment rises, but then a brave soul stands up and projects her voice. Soon, more follow.

When the Polish anthem begins, *Jeszcze Polska nie zginęła*, Poland is Not Yet Lost, an anthem I know well, I start to stand up, but Helena's restraining hand compels me to sit down.

"Shush!" she warns with a finger across her lips. "It's not our turn yet!"

"Why?" I wonder.

"You wait. You'll see," she whispers.

And, of course, I shush.

Standing up is not so easy for me. My feet don't quite reach the floor and I scoot back into my chair with some difficulty. I am, of course, very small for my age. Because of my small size and my lack of hair, the Swedish social worker who later works with us refugees, insults me terribly when she classifies me as a five-year-old boy.

When the Polish anthem ends, the women around me, evidently the Zionist component, rise to sing, and I manage to scoot off my chair again and join them. The sad, stirring tune and the foreign words are completely new to me. But they pierce me with sharp and electrifying intensity. "What was that song?" I ask Helena who stands beside me.

"That," she explains, "was *HaTikva*, the national anthem of the Jews. *HaTikva* is Hebrew for 'The Hope.' The song is about the hope that we Jews have of returning to our home in Palestine and in Jerusalem to be a nation, to return home, to rebuild the home that we lost two thousand years ago. The home we have never forgotten."

It is May of 1945. World War II had not yet ended. The place is Morup in the agricultural province of Halland in Sweden. And all of a sudden I know that I have to join in the longing and the dream to fulfil the hope of *HaTikva*.

But it is more. In that moment in Halland, a new poignant reality presents itself. It is a mental picture that will reconfigure not only my emotional life but also reconstruct my husband John's life, and the futures of our children and grandchildren.

I didn't know it then, of course, but that moment of melodies started my lifelong search for a stable and somehow unified personhood. In today's global village, where it is rather "in" to be "out", do we still need that place that is home, or can home shift as

grandchildren would visit—places where they would continue to belong, belong in a way that I knew I never could.

Now, as I move up the stairs, I see a piece of dirty paper on the step in front of me and without much thought, I pick it up and move on to the fifth floor. I drag my feet walking slowly on my way to the math lesson that I particularly dislike. I notice that the mend in my stocking has given way again to allow the skin of my knee to show. I had long since given up trying to look or act like the others, but this unmended stocking, right now, right there in front of me makes me feel particularly unkempt. Like the greasy piece of paper sticking to my fingers, it underlines my sense of outsiderness and disarray. At this time in my life, I own only two skirts and they are the wrong kind. My dark hair never stays in place.

On these stairs, I so often wish that I could disappear. Sometimes, I just want to fade away into one of the Carl Larson pictures, but the girls in those murals, too, are lovely, contented, and purposeful. They too, are pieces in an orderly historical puzzle where there is no space mapped out for me.

When I get to the fifth floor, I walk over to the large waste can and throw in the oily paper I had picked up on the stairs. I am just about to turn left for room 506, when I feel a tap on my shoulder.

There stands the teacher—a short, dark-haired, rather plump lady. To this day I don't know her name. She has never taught in any of the classes I had at *Nya Elementar*. I don't know what subjects she taught; what her disciplinary strategies might have been, what her pedagogical outlook was, or what kinds of lesson plans she might have preferred. Yet, in half a minute, this one teacher has managed to place herself as a driving force and a beacon of blessed tidings for me. It is at this moment that I make my career choice, a choice that will serve me meaningfully for over 47 years.

"I want to tell you something," the teacher says and looks straight into my eyes. "And I want you to listen carefully because whether you know it or not, this is not a small matter. I have been standing here at every recess watching hundreds of girls walking up these stairs. That piece of paper has been there all day. I know because I put it there. Of all the girls who have walked up these stairs you were the only one who picked it up to throw it away." Then the teacher touches my cheek. "You are a special girl, little, dark, foreign bird. Don't ever forget that. Now go to your class."

So, I turn left and walk to class, but my step is lighter now, and for the first time at *Nya Elementar* I hold my head high. Somehow, life is good. Suddenly, if only for just a few minutes, I belong. Somehow, I have just been handed the ticket to belonging.

I have kept the face of that unknown teacher in my mind and I have remembered how vital each word said by a teacher can be.

THOUGHTS OF A VERY CHILDISH
SIXTEEN-YEAR-OLD

In 1952, I am at the end of my fifteenth year. I will be sixteen as soon as I arrive in America. Do I really have to go? Honestly, I can't believe it. Of course I have always known that it was going to happen; but now it is really happening, and there is nothing I can do about it. How can I possibly leave Sweden? I have worked so hard at becoming a Swedish girl. And now I am a Swedish girl. Truly, I am a real Swedish girl. Yes, yes, I know that I can never be blond, and I can never be tall, but that doesn't really matter, does it? I can curtsy like any good Swedish girl does, and by now, I speak a beautiful Swedish without the slightest trace of an accent. My favorite author is Selma Lagerlöf, and I have read *Nils Holgerson's Wonderful Journey* so many times that I almost know it by heart, and I have promised myself that one day, when I am grown up, I will make the Nils Holgerson journey all across the length and breadth of Sweden, just like Nils did on the back of a goose, while I, of course, will travel on trains. I know the Swedish national anthem by heart. I can clasp my fingers together and recite *The Lord's Prayer* in evocative Swedish. I have earned straight As in the required Lutheran Christianity course, even though, to be honest now, I feel terribly guilty about having attended this class because, of course, I am Jewish and I shouldn't be taking such a class, and if I had been completely honest, I would have gone to the principal and asked for an exemption from the class, but I hadn't done that! And why not? Mostly because I didn't want to call attention to myself, but to tell the truth, it was quite fascinating to learn exactly what Swedish Christian Lutherans believe, and why they believe it, and why, on earth, they would think that this nice Rabbi, who had wandered around the sea of Galilee saying good things, was God.

My favorite king from Swedish history is Gustav Adolph the 12th. He was the founder of my city, Göteborg. My favorite queen is Gustav Adolph's daughter, Queen Kristina, even though she rebelled against her dad, became a Catholic, and moved to Rome— never mind, she was a gutsy girl and I love her like I love the midnight sun, and the craggy mountains, and the blue-yellow flag.

It has taken me six years to transform myself into this Swedish girl, who has Swedish friends, who dreams in Swedish and has read the *Kullla-Gulla* books, and has learned to smile the soft and slow Swedish smile, who rides to school on a Swedish bike that she has bought with her own money earned by picking tomatoes and cucumbers at Gurk-Svenson's farm during her summer vacation, and she knows nothing absolutely nothing, zero, nil, zilch, about America. Except that she has found some books in the library— some books that she read, translated into Swedish, of course, but they were by an American author. His name is Mark Twain, and I love his books more than anything in the world—*Tom Sawyer* and *Huckleberry Finn*. They were Americans—but very long ago when they still had slaves in America. What a horrible thing to have slaves.

I don't want to go to America. America is huge and scary. One of their great cities is Chicago, and it is full of gangsters, and I will have to travel on a train that goes right through that city of thugs.

And it even stops there, so an American gangster might kill me. Well, that way I wouldn't have to worry about learning English, but it does seem crazy to have survived a German concentration camp just to get killed by an American gangster.

Sweden is a small country, a safe country. The national anthem is about the sun, blue skies, and green meadows. I don't want to leave Sweden, but of course, I have no say in this matter. The adults in my life have decided. I have to go. Those are the rules. I have an aunt and uncle in America. People must go and live with their closest relatives. I have no relatives in Sweden. Helena promised my father that as soon as the war was over, and if we survived, she would send me to my aunt in America.

I love Helena so much. She and Kuba have settled in Sweden and now they have my little brother, Olek. I love my little brother, though he, of course, is not my real brother. Will I ever see them again? America is so far away. I am terrified like I was during the war. Except then everyone was afraid and now I am the only one. I am by myself on an island of fear, and the water around the island is black. In my dreams, the Nazi soldiers are chasing me, and I wake up in cold sweat.

Helena has talked to the principal of my school and he has told her that if I really hate America and want to return, they will take me back. "That girl is always welcome," he said.

I am surprised and happy because my school, *Flickorna's Högre Alemena Läroverk,* was not easy to get into. And I have been so happy there, and I was so glad to get out of the silly, fancy *Nya Elementar. Flickorna's Högre Alemena Läroverk* is the "smart, hard-working girls' school", and I am one of those hard-working, smart, Swedish girls. Aren't I?

Here, in my new school, we are allowed to talk about money and ask someone how much something costs. I have discovered that rich people don't ever talk about money. They think it's impolite. That's what I learned at *Nya Elementar.*

"You are lucky," the Swedish counselor to America tells me as he hands me my new D.P. passport. "America just made some new laws that allow stateless people like you to come. Not everyone is so lucky, you know. Your native country, Poland, has allowed you to give up your Polish citizenship and you are still one year away from being able to apply for Swedish citizenship, so now you are state-less—a D.P., a displaced person, and you can start a new life in America—lucky girl! Good luck!"

He smiles at me, and I say *"Tack så mycket,"* (Thank You) and do my Swedish curtsy, but I don't want to start a new life. I have just created this life here—my Swedish life. I don't want to leave it. I have had two years of school English, but the lessons were just one hour twice a week. I have learned Swedish, and I know that learning a language is not so easy—not if you really want to learn it the way I have learned Swedish, so that the language sings inside of you.

I sit in my Swedish history class and I cannot concentrate on the lesson, because, of course, all this is no longer important. Yes, I still love Swedish history, but my mind right now is full of worry. How will I ever know how to write a composition in English? To pass an exam in English? To answer teachers' questions in English? Am I going to have to start in first grade again in America like I had to do in Sweden? How can I ever make friends if I can't talk to them? Can I create a new person—a new American girl? Do I want to?

They tell me that in America, boys and girls go to school together. I know nothing about boys. The few I have met when I worked at Gurk-Svensons, the place where I picked cucumbers during summer vacations, had hair on their arms and talked with funny deep voices.

I wish I could take someone with me. Someone who knows me just a little bit. Someone who could remember Sweden together with me. Maybe just a little dog or a little cat, who would know me and remember me as the Swedish self I have turned myself into, the Swedish self that I am supposed to leave behind. What a silly thought! I am almost sixteen years old. I shouldn't be having such silly thoughts.

What can I be in America? What can I ever become?

LEAVING

January 1952. I stand on the deck of the *Gripsholm*. I can still see all of them down below on the quayside here to see me off. My whole world is down there on the ground. They look smaller from my perch up on the second deck, and I wonder if they can see me. Of course Helena in her black Persian lamb coat sees me. She waves. Then she picks up Olek, who is four years old, and he, too, waves.

My heart twists. I am really leaving my baby brother, my darling little baby, whose diapers I had changed and for whom I had sung lullabies as he snuggled up to sleep. Kuba looks frozen. He doesn't wave. I know that he is cold and would like to go home, and there, in a group, are my girlfriends. I hadn't expected all of them to come. They stand together. Liljan, trenchcoat-dressed like me, her beautiful, straight blond hair tied back in a long braid. She is crying. She had started out as my greatest challenger for the History Award, and had later become my closest friend. The others just look bewildered. They are all bundled up against the cold. I know that Birgitta, who is just wearing a heavy sweater, is the one who must feel the cold in the worst possible way, and I am grateful to her for coming to see me off. The wind is ferocious, and there they are—all waving. My friends, the brainy girls of second class *Flickläroverket*. Ingrid, Ella-Britt, Liljan, Birgitta, Greta, and Sigrid. These are not the beauties of the class. Neither are they the accomplished athletes. They are the good students. The literature and history buffs. Sweden's future career women, ambitious, hard-working girls, so different from the girls of *Nya Elementar*.

A wave of contentment washes over me. I have finally made good friends, and then just as suddenly? the wave recedes. I know that I am losing the friendships that I had worked so hard to obtain and keep. Going to America is like going to the moon. Does anyone ever come back? How could I afford it?

Fear bores through me like a dentist's drill. I am leaving friendship, leaving security. Leaving everything I have ever known. Leaving everything I have ever loved. Leaving for what? Anxiety gnaws at my innards. My friends on the quay wave. I wave back.

The wind is strong and bitingly cold. I shiver in spite of my new trench coat, the same trench coat that I had considered stylishly appropriate just a week earlier. Now, it is just heavy and school-girlishly juvenile. I am supposed to be and act grown up, but I feel infantile, a lost child on her way to nowhere. My feet are blocks of ice.

Here up on the deck, all around me are groups of passengers, families, couples, and groups of friends traveling together. Everyone seems excited. Everyone seems to know where they are going, and why they are going there. Everywhere there are smiles of expectancy, at the process of starting an adventure, while I am about to abandon a life chapter that I had just barely started to read correctly.

I feel trapped in a bubble of aloneness. I am once again nobody's person, a solitary fragment drifting in the wind in my new, now inappropriate trench coat. On my head is my slanted school beret. This was a fine outfit for my Swedish schoolgirl life just a few days ago. Now it seems all wrong and oddly misplaced.

How can a few days make such a difference? The people here on deck are dressed in fur-lined jackets. The women wear stylish trousers. Long woolen scarves flutter everywhere. Why hadn't I realized that a scarf would be necessary?

I stare until the ship moves and the forms I know grow smaller and disappear in the fog.

TWO WEEKS AT SEA

I spend about a third of my journey to America on deck leaning over the railing in a mostly unsuccessful attempt to puke. It is midwinter and the seas are stormy. I frequently visit Stina, the ship's friendly Swedish nurse. I am not sure that what I really want from her is medical advice or whether I just want to chat in Swedish. Stina is in her twenties. She laughs easily, wears a starched nurse's uniform—a blue dress and over it an unbelievably and completely snow-white apron. How on earth does she keep it so spotlessly white? Her blond curls bounce as she shakes her head and firmly admonishes me about how to swallow the pills.

I know that I am speaking Swedish for the last time in my life and I relish the taste of each word as it touches my tongue. I have lost languages before: Polish, Yiddish, German. I know how this happens, and I know that there is a taste of longing forever lasting in one's throat. Going to America is going to the moon. It is true that some people do return, but they are the rich, the important, and the famous. I will surely never be one of them. So who am I going to be in that strange new place over there on the other side of this dreadful ocean?

"Breathe deeply," Stina tells me. "Don't stay in your room. Get out on the deck and get some fresh air. Talk to people. Get in the swimming pool."

The *Gripsholm* is a luxury liner. Decks are connected by beautiful wooden stairways. There is a swimming pool, a cinema, and inviting lounges. In the dining room, I am surrounded by Polish refugees and almost, without my taking notice of it, my Polish returns.

Everyone I meet on the *Gripsholm* has relatives somewhere in the United States. I had not talked Polish for several years. In Sweden, we had followed the typical immigrant pattern. First, Helena and I spoke Polish. Then she spoke Polish and I answered in Swedish. Eventually, after Kuba's arrival, we all switched to Swedish. But here, on the *Gripsholm,* when my Polish suddenly and surprisingly bounces back, I am grateful. At least I will be able to talk to my relatives when I meet them.

There are lessons in English offered on the boat and I attend. I learn that, "A horse is an animal with four legs." And I wonder just how useful a sentence like this might prove to be. I also learn to say, "I don't speak much English. Could you please repeat that," as well as, "Could you speak more slowly?"

The linguist in me wonders of what use those sentences might be if I really didn't know the words of the speaker. What did it matter if they repeated or spoke more slowly? Later, I notice that when you don't understand what people are saying, the speakers tend to raise their voices. As if not knowing a language somehow might make you deaf. I promise myself that I will never do that to anyone.

We watch a movie, staring Dorothy Lamour. Everyone in my group is completely enchanted. *Sliczna dziewczynka, sliczna dziewczynka* (what a gorgeous girl) is the murmur that makes it around the theater. But I just want to hold on to Swedish a while longer, just a little bit longer, just two more weeks of pretending to be a Swedish girl. Let me relish each day. Let me think in Swedish, move in Swedish, dress in Swedish, even throw up in Swedish. Up there, on the Swedish deck, that does seem possible.

I have a room to myself, and I sleep on the bottom half of a bunk bed. No one sleeps on the top bunk. The boat stops in Bremerhaven, where German passengers board the ship.

Among the Polish refugees on board there is palpable tension. One of the new arrivals is a German lady who is to become my roommate. It is the first time, after the war, that I have been in such proximity to a real German person. My back crawls with apprehension. *She is just a person,* I tell myself. *But where was she seven years ago? Where was she ten years ago? Where was she when I was in Ravensbrück?*

She seems a pleasant enough lady in her 30s or 40s, maybe 50s? I can't tell with grown-ups. She has brown hair rolled back in a chignon, wears blouses with lace frills around her collar, and flannel pajamas. She asks what my name is. I smile and shake my head, pretending that I don't understand German. How I hate the sound of that language. Its guttural resonance makes my skin crawl. She tries English, and again I shake my head. Please, I just don't want to talk to her.

Later in life, I will regret the opportunity. I could have gotten to know her. Maybe she was a lady with an interesting story—maybe even a good story, but now we just smile at one another. I know that my smile is more a grin than a smile, but that will have to do right now.

"*Jag talar bara Svenska,*" (I speak only Swedish) I tell her, infusing the false pride with accents of superiority. We are, after all, on a Swedish ship. I can permit myself this monolinguistic elitism.

At night, I get up to throw up into a paper bag, provided for that specific purpose, and the German lady's voice is solicitous when she asks about my health. I mumble something that I hope sounds as a response, but I want to scream at her: "So now you worry about my health! Some joke! Not so long ago, you just barely missed the chance to kill me, and now you inquire about my health."

I know that this is nuts. I know that this is not fair. I know nothing about this woman. Perhaps she was one of the good Germans. Maybe she was one of those who married a Jew. Maybe she hid Jews in her basement. Maybe she was in a concentration camp, too. These things are all possibilities, but now, I just want to stay out of her way.

I become part of a Polish-Jewish refuge group. Among them there is Withold Cohn. He is nineteen years old and is traveling with his mother. At the swimming pool he seems to admire my shape in a bathing suit, but we are both too awkward for any advance. He has been accepted to Lincoln College somewhere in the East. He is just as nervous as I am.

"How am I going to be able to read an American text book?" he wonders. "How am I going to write an essay in English?"

Of course, I sympathize, but I am also jealous. He has been accepted to something. That means he has a future. A place somewhere is held for him, while I am traveling through limbo to yet another indeterminate state. Also, he is traveling with his mother, while I wallow in isolation. He and his mother will be able to talk to each other about Sweden. In the group of refugees, there are also the Bronskis, an older couple, who will join Mr. Bronski's brother in a linen business in Chicago.

"So, you are going to be with relatives in Evansville, Indiana," Mr. Bronksi says. "Too bad really. A pretty and smart girl like you. Some rich Jewish family in New York would have been happy to adopt you. Too bad you have those relatives. Well, I suppose you'll make the best of it!"

It's really the first time I envision myself as an orphan desirable for adoption. Is that really what I am, and how would I make myself worthy of such a family? What would they expect? What do my relatives expect? Will I live up to their expectations? What does "making the best of it" mean?

There is a young couple, Layla and Rubin. They walk the decks holding hands. Layla wears her dark hair tied back in a long ponytail. She dresses in stylish wool slacks and tight turtleneck sweaters that accentuate her womanly bust line. I think that she is beautiful. She tells me that she is scared but excited. "We will be starting our new lives together in a new land," she says.

"What is it like to be married?" I ask her.

"I am just finding out," she says. "I am not always happy about it. There are times when I think I should have waited. Given myself a chance to meet American men, you know."

I am surprised. I hadn't expected that kind of an answer, but I recognize and honor the realism it implies. Layla looks at me, and laughs. "Wash your face with Ivory soap every day," she says, demonstrating with a circling gesture on her face how it should be done. "And you too will be married one of these days!"

The ship stops in Halifax, Canada, where my German roommate disembarks. We have not exchanged a single word, and I am glad to see her go. And then we are headed for New York. In the middle of the night, I hear the sound of a horn. The hallways are crowded. People stream upward toward the decks. "The statue of liberty! Come to see her. There is the statue of liberty."

I rub sleep out of my eyes and stumble up the stairs. Everyone is on deck. The sky is a black velvet pincushion stuck with millions of diamond pinhead stars, and before us stands the myth in stone just like I have always imagined her in floodlit majesty! She is supposed to be welcoming me with her outstretched arm and her lighted torch, but she doesn't strike me as the welcoming mother. Instead, she is a figure of might and glory, the kind of power I find foreboding. How, on earth, am I to fit into this?

Powerlessness wraps itself around me. I have read her poem. I know that a Jewish woman, Emma Lazarus, had written it "the wretched refuse of your teeming shore." I am that wretched refuse. The insult cuts to the bone. I will have to prove otherwise to this metal lady. How long will I be that "wretched refuse?" We are people on this boat, and we are not wretched refuse. Who are you to tell us we are wretched? We come to give not to take. We are the stories of the world. We bring treasure!

My uncle Moshe and cousin Ben will be there to meet me. How will I recognize them among all these people? Luckily they find me. I dig out a vague memory of my uncle. I remember him from Poland as a dapper young man. Here in America, he looks wilted and diminished. I know that he, his wife, and small daughter survived the war on false papers in Warsaw.

After the war, he served as a judge in Warsaw, but somehow he had gotten in trouble with the communist regime and had fled to Canada. With his family, he had immigrated to the USA just a year earlier. I am to stay with his family before I start the journey to Evansville, Indiana, where my aunt, uncle, and cousin live. Cousin Ben I had never previously met. They kiss me on both cheeks, and take my suitcases. I follow them in a state of complete bewilderment. *There is no point in thinking*, I tell myself. *Just let things happen.*

"Maybe she would look better if she put on some lipstick," Ben says to Moshe in Yiddish, which I wish that I couldn't understand, but of course, I do.

"Welcome to America," someone says.

PART 3
NEWCOMER IN AMERICA

BECOMING AN AMERICAN GIRL

I never got to know her first name. For me, she will always be "Dean Long." In Swedish the word *lång* (pronounced "long") means "tall," and indeed this lady is tall. That's the first thing I notice about her. Her steel gray hair is piled on top of her head in an impressive bun, which only adds to her striking figure. Her eyes are deep blue. She is wearing a gray suit. The skirt is pencil slim. The blouse peeking out from under her suit jacket is colorful. A blue cameo pin, framed in gold, graces the lapel of her jacket.

As she steps out from behind her desk, I notice that she is wearing high-heeled pumps that show off slim ankles. She is in charge of my destiny, and I am ready to worship her. She stands behind her desk as she greets us, but she comes forward, and amazingly moves towards me rather than towards Uncle Ben. "Hello, there, Natalie," she says and her voice rings with possibility. "Welcome to Bosse High School."

And this is how I am born and baptized into my new American self. I have left my real name, Natalia Chojnacka, in the front office downstairs. The clerk looked at it without even trying to pronounce it. She had given me a bewildered look and sent us on upstairs, where the sign on the door proclaimed 'Dean of Girls.'

The walk up those American stairs turns out to be crucial for my new identity. On those stairs, I make the decision to call myself "Boksenberg," using my uncle's family name as mine.

In my ears, at the moment, Boksenberg, in spite of its length, just seems more normal than my own evidently totally impossible Chojnacka. At any rate, it is a possible if not a perfect name for this new American self that I am now just trying out. After all, I have already changed names several times during my life, and this change, right now, seems a sensible decision. As I face Dean Long, she quite perfunctorily baptizes me and Americanizes me into "Natalie."

At this moment, in Dean Long's office, I am Natalie Boksenberg, an American girl in the making, very half-baked certainly, but nevertheless a vague imprint of what is to be.

Dean Long gives me her focused attention, which in turn gives me the courage to present myself.

"I am sixteen years old," I tell her, "and I want to be in high school."

This is as far as Uncle Ben is willing to allow me before he, my designated adult protector, assumes center stage. "I have been trying to explain to my niece," he says. "I have been trying to tell her." His voice is measured and purposeful. "I have been trying to clarify that one cannot start in high school. But she will not understand. She doesn't know English. She doesn't know the American system or the American curriculum.

I have been trying to tell her that she must start in the first grade—like I did when I first came to this country. The teachers will gradually promote her through the grades as she learns the language. It will, of course, take a year or two, but she is a young person. As she grows older, two years or so make no difference, but she is a stubborn girl and she will not understand." Uncle Ben grows excited. His gold-rimmed glasses slide down on his now perspiring nose and he straightens these before continuing. "I and her dear aunt, my wife, have had many discussions about all this, but she insisted that I bring her here to high school, so that she could hear it from the proper authorities. I am so sorry that we have taken up your time. You have my sincere apology, Dean Long."

Dean Long is silent. She moves behind her desk, where she becomes an immovable statue of ultimate authority. She gives Uncle Ben a steely look. She turns her eyes toward me and I don't dare to believe it, but do I really perceive the light of sympathy? Again, she moves her gaze toward Uncle Ben. Her gaze grows implacable and steady. "Natalie needs to be with youngsters her own age."

I want to fall on the ground and kiss her feet, and I will surely go to my grave blessing her name.

POPPING ALONG IN AMERICA

The counselor at Bosse High School enrolls me in four different classes of English. The most important one is advanced composition taught by Miss Stautenberg, who daily presents us with grammar and punctuation exercises.

In her class, I learn that American English doesn't just have to be learned. It also has to be diagrammed on carefully understood structures where words assume positions on straight or slanted lines as well as on elevated platforms. A whole clause used as an object goes on stilts in the object slot, never to be confused with the complement. I find the diagramming a fascinating game and soon practice it with pleasurable conformity. I also learn the difference between phrase and clause. Diagramming has order and logic. Spelling, however, eludes me.

"Just look at the word," I am admonished. "Does it look right?"

I can't tell. All the words look right, or for that matter, all the words look wrong to me. I am used to spelling by sound, and the sounds and letters in English very often don't go together. What does the "w" do in "write?" And why isn't it also in "right?" Why do you spell "Sally" with two l's, but "salary" with only one? Why do "believe" and "receive" sound the same but look different on paper? And why do "bed" and "bread" both have the same "e" sound but are spelled differently?

Each week, Miss Stautenberg also assigns us a vocabulary list. I learn the meanings of words like "primogeniture," "pusillanimous," "altruistic," "inchoate" and "solipsism", and I discover, much to my surprise, that Uncle Ben doesn't know the meanings of these words. Suddenly, I am one up on Uncle Ben! I gloat with much satisfaction.

Most of the time, I find the explanations in the Webster's English dictionary too complicated, but my Swedish/English lexicon saves me.

The guidance counselor also assigns me to English as well as American Literature. In these classes, I barely understand what is going on. Mostly I am dazed, but, nevertheless, I am enchanted. I learn that Mark Twain, whose work I had loved in Swedish translation, is actually a famous American writer. The knowledge that I already know one famous American writer, and that I actually had discovered him all on my own in a library in Sweden, now so far away, reassures me. I also realize that Evansville, Indiana, where I now live, is located on the Ohio River.

"Is this the place where Eliza crosses from Kentucky to Indiana in *Uncle Tom's Cabin?*" I ask. Nobody knows what I am talking about.

The guidance counselor also assigns me to a class in Home Economics. "Just to lighten your load," she tells me.

The Home Economics class is taught by Miss B. She tells us that her name is hard to pronounce, and since other things in the course might grow complicated, we might as well just stick to "B" and not worry about her real name. I sympathize, and am instantly charmed by Miss B, a pleasantly rounded lady dressed in loose, comfortable-looking caftan style dresses. I wonder how she can be so casual about her name. I have already undergone three name changes in my life, and each time it seemed I had to shed an identity and take on quite a different one.

Twelve very large athletes attend the Home Economics class and soon tell me that they are there for "at least one easy credit." I am the only girl in the class. For a while, I feel discounted and out of place with these enormously overgrown guys. But soon, I begin to feel a certain kinship with them. After all, I am there for the same easy-class reason. The guys are nice to me, treating me like a lost little sister. Miss B. has questions written up on the board, and we spend most of our class periods, answering those questions in writing. The answers are to be found in various cookbooks that we locate on the shelves. We each also each have a textbook, *The Real Economy of Home Economics*.

As the curriculum proceeds, I learn the subtle difference in the meaning of words like "fry," "stir-fry," "sauté," "deep-fry" and "brown." We learn how to deep-fry chicken, and how to peel potatoes the right way, and how to set the table. Sometimes there seems to be a waste of many leftovers. Occasionally, a memory of potato peeling in the ghetto where each too deeply cut wasted skin was severely criticized, floats up in my mind where I promptly squash it.

"A Polish family could live off the things that go into an American garbage can," Aunt Dora tells me.

I know what she is talking about, but I promptly erase all these thoughts from my consciousness. I am too busy trying to become an American girl. In certain ways this process is easier than I thought it would be. The girls in America dress like grown-up women. They paint their nails and wear lipstick. They wear tight sweaters that are completed at the neckline by little white collars, and fastened at the throat by small bouquets of artificial flowers.

When I first meet these girls, I assume that since they look so grown up, they must surely also be very smart, but I soon discover that I don't have much to fear on that score, and that is a great relief. On the other hand, there are some most peculiar customs that give me a hard time. The girls change clothes every day. Why, I wonder? Surely their clothes don't get dirty so fast and so often. I own two skirts and two sweaters. I wear one outfit until it gets dirty, and then while I wash one, I wear the other one.

Later, my new friend, Julie, explains the system. "It makes you more attractive for the boys," she says. "You see, one has school clothes and home clothes. The minute you get home, you take off your school clothes and hang them up in the closet. You put on your home clothes that are not nearly as nice as the school clothes. You can wear those same home clothes all the time, but your school clothes must be different every single day. You must have at least five school outfits or if you only have four, you could possibly wear the same thing on Monday and on Thursday."

It takes me a while to notice that Julie, who is so well-versed in these rules of conduct, is, herself, also a bit different. She wears Mary-Jane soft shoes with nylon stockings, and not the Oxfords with rolled bobby sox like all the others. Is Julie's difference the reason she is the only one who dares to befriend me? I discover that she is a talented actress. She introduces me to the Thespians at Bosse High School, and suddenly I start making more friends.

In Home Economics, we have a bit of an accident. Some soup boils over and one of the guys burns his hand. All activity stops, as Len, over his loud protests, is sent to the nurse's office.

"We should do something lighter today," Miss B. says. "I know what we are going to do. Let's teach Natalie how to make popcorn."

SCHOOL GIRL, DEALING WITH NUMBERS

I move toward my locker on the third floor. I have lived in Evansville, Indiana for almost a year, and much of the time, I do my thinking in English, but I have noticed that whenever numbers are used, I automatically switch to Swedish, and then translate the numbers to English. I have been told that this is how the language-learning process works. People seem to switch to the language in which they learned things like the multiplication table in the language that first taught them these terms.

I am wearing a new American outfit, gray skirt and a yellow turtleneck sweater. On my feet are the required Oxfords with the accompanying rolled-down bobby socks. These are all fairly new acquisitions, mostly bought with the money I earned during the summer's babysitting. I still don't dare to shop for clothes on my own, and Aunt Dora accompanies me to the big downtown department stores, Lerner or Straus on Main Street. Aunt Dora has a good eye for clothes and I mostly follow her advice. My waistline is 22 inches—a far cry from Scarlet O'Hara's seventeen , which I think is required for a real American girlhood.

An American girl also has to shave off the hair both on her legs and in her armpits. She has to spray herself with deodorant, and she chews *Juicy Fruit* gum, so that she won't have bad breath. Bad breath and body odor are problems that seem to be of great trouble for Americans. I never heard of these problems in Europe. Also, an American girl must set her hair in bobby-pin curls every night. She must wear lipstick that improbably either matches or attractively contrasts with her clothes.

Julie has explained all this to me. She has also told me that a sweater should be snug, but not too tight. "You will know that your sweater is too tight if boys give you a leery look," she says, "If your sweater is just nice and snug, they will look too, but their looks will be approving. You'll see."

An American girl is expected to be "friendly", which means that you should smile a lot and say, "Hi," to everyone. There seems to be a big difference between being "friendly" and being "a friend." These things confuse me.

Ann keeps a mountain of comic books on the floor. From the Archie and Veronica comic books, I learn to say that appropriate "Hi," which is pronounced *"heye"* like in *"eye"* and not *"hee"* as in *"see"* as I had originally assumed.

"The letter "i" always says its name," I am told. It's not true actually. It seems to stick to a short "e" in words like "it" or "bit."

My English has gotten a lot better, but I still always seem to translate. From what to what? I am never quite sure. I have now been through Polish, German, Yiddish, and Swedish. Only Swedish was my love, but now it seems to be leaking out of me, away from my brain and nothing has yet taken its place. I am floating in a bewildering linguistic limbo, and I wish that I could find my way out of it.

I would love to get a weekend job in one of those Main Street stores, but I am afraid that my English is still not good enough. I can read my school textbooks, but the thought of addressing customers in a commercial setting terrifies me.

Money is becoming a problem. When I first arrived, Uncle Ben offered me a weekly allowance of three dollars. He stuck to this for some months, but then he stopped. Has he just forgotten, or am I now supposed to have found a way of making my own money? I am too embarrassed to ask. I have saved some money, and I keep it in an envelope under my socks and underpants.

I know that I am a lot of trouble to my American family. They paid for the ticket that brought me. I shouldn't have insisted on bringing my bike. It must have been very expensive to have it brought all the way, but in Sweden I had seen my bike as a serious means of transportation.

Here in Evansville, Indiana, in the 1950s only small children ride bikes. After a while, I stop riding it to school. Most students come on the bus, but I get car sick, so I walk to school. Some students have cars of their own. You can drive a car when you are sixteen in America. One girl, Ruthie, drives a big white Buick. I will have to learn to drive. It's a requirement for graduation, but my family doesn't have a car and I am terrified of the whole idea of driving. The Driver Education teacher had been very straightforward: "Don't forget that when you hold the steering wheel and step on the clutch and gas, you are handling a lethal instrument."

I had to look up the word "lethal." Why would anyone want to drive?

My aunt and uncle belong to a Reform Synagogue. They call their synagogue a Temple. It's a very strange place. If I didn't know any better, I would think that they belonged to a church. The men and women sit together. Nobody wears a prayer shawl or a head covering. They say their prayers in English with a few bits of the familiar Hebrew just thrown in here and there. There is also a choir that sings. The rabbi wears a weird churchy outfit. The Jews here seem not to know about what happened in Europe. Perhaps they really don't want to know. It scares them, and I can understand that. It scares me too and during the daytime, I blot out the nightmares, in which the Nazi soldiers chase me. In Sweden the nightmares had stopped a few years ago, but now they are all back.

I love school, and I know that school is my road to adulthood and to independence. If I just make it through this school, I will be able to go to college. In college, I will learn a profession, and then I will finally be an adult. I won't have to depend on anyone. I won't have to be grateful. I hate to be grateful. I know that I am supposed to be grateful to the relatives who have taken me in; grateful to the Polish family who kept me for a while; grateful to Helena who saved my life; grateful to Sweden for allowing me to live there and go to school; grateful to Fru Erlander who put me into one of the best schools; grateful to God who has made me a Jew.

Oh, dear God, sometimes I get so tired of it all. I want to stop having to be grateful. I want to be grown up. I want to be independent. I will keep God, I suppose. I decide that everyone must be grateful for life. I wonder what made God create people. Julie and I talk about it at night when she drives me home from play rehearsals. We decide that God must have been lonely. That was probably why he created people. Suddenly from nowhere, I remember what my grandmother had once told me: *"Tikkun Olam"* (repairing the world).

"We are here to help God make the world better," I tell Julie.

She seems favorably inclined to the idea and suggests: "Maybe God is a she." We both break out in giggles over the impossibility of such an idea.

School is easy here compared to school in Sweden. The teachers are nice and, yes, "friendly" in the American way. I used to be terrible in sports, which was a real handicap in Sweden. Here, the gym teacher just throws a ball to us, points to the basket on the wall, and says, "Play, girls!" And the girls do, but no one seems to take the game seriously, and one need only to say, "Period!" or "The witch is visiting," to be excused and be allowed to sit out on the side and watch. I sit and watch a lot and I practice the irregular verbs:

"Go, went, gone"; "dive, dove" (is it "dived" or "diven"?); "sneak, snuck, snuck" or did she say that it was really "sneaked, sneaked"?

Ahead of me in the hallway, three girls walk together, their arms circling around one another. All three are wearing their crinolines and together they block the entire hallway. A guy passes me and his careful once-over look caresses and pleases me. His look does not seem leery. I guess I got the snugness right. Of course this is not THE boy for whom I long, Mike, who sits next to me in French class. He is cool, and smart, and sophisticated, and I would give a lot for a glance from him, but I know that his eyes are on Carolyn, and who can blame him? Carolyn looks like Elizabeth Taylor. Carolyn gets the romantic lead in every play.

I have become a Thespian. On Thursdays, we Thespians wear gigantic letter Ts across our chests to signal our status and our belonging. It wasn't easy to become a Thespian. The wonderful Miss Cupp held demanding and competitive tryouts in room 163. Miss Cupp, who has beautiful red hair and always wears sexy dresses and very high-heeled shoes, teaches speech and drama. I will try to get into one of her classes next semester.

This year, I heard her read *The Littlest Angel* to an assembly and even though Christmas, of course, is not my holiday I allow myself to melt into her melodic performance. Our chosen drama for performance this semester is *The Barretts of Wimpole Street*. Carolyn, naturally, has the lead, as Elizabeth Barrett, but Miss Cupp has chosen me to play the part of Henrietta, Elizabeth's rebellious sister, even though I can barely produce an American accent and much less a British one.

To tell the truth, I can barely notice the difference that everyone is making such a fuss about. Miss Cupp also picks me to play Mary in the Christmas pageant. All I would have to do is sit there smiling with a baby doll on my lap, while the angels all around me sing. It seems so sweet and romantic, but really it isn't a thing for a Jewish girl to do, and when Uncle Ben throws a fit and forbids me to take the part, I grumble, but really I know he is right this time.

I love the lockers. A place of my own, where I can keep anything I want to keep. The school provides me with wonderful textbooks, and nobody else can use my locker. I can decorate it any way I want to. I can put anything I want in it—an extra sweater, my gym clothes, a mirror, or a dead body. I laugh at the thought.

In Sweden, I had a desk that opened up where I kept my books and where there was a hole for the inkwell, before I got my treasured fountain pen, but there were desk inspections and you were in serious trouble if you didn't keep your desk tidy. Here I can make any mess I want to in my locker. It is my private place. I turn the lock to open my locker with my own private combination.

I say the numbers and twirl the lock backwards and forwards, and magically the locker opens up for me, but then I become aware of something that has never happened before, and I wasn't even thinking about it. As I twirled the lock I had said the numbers in English. I had said them very clearly 63-84-63. And then I said them out loud in English. I wasn't translating from the Swedish. How very strange.

Maybe, I am becoming an American girl after all.

OF COWS AND COWARDS

"Cowards die many times before their deaths.
The valiant never taste of death but once.
Of all the wonders that I yet have heard,
It seems to me most strange that men should fear,
Seeing that death, a necessary end,
Will come when it will come."
- Shakespeare, *Julius Caesar*, Act 2 Scene 2

Miss Andersen reads the passage from *Julius Caesar* in her usually dramatic voice. She infuses her reading with the kind of passion that connotes both the intrinsic tragedy and the underlying wisdom of the text. Miss Andersen is not conventionally pretty. Her front teeth protrude a bit too much. Her hair is frizzy, surrounding her face with a perpetually uncombed halo. The blue-framed glasses on her nose are always a bit crooked, but once her voice projects itself on the class, she becomes totally enchanting.

I love her voice. The wonder of it wraps me in harmony, and I think that I understand what she is reading even though, later in study hall, when I look the words up in my Swedish/English dictionary, I realize that I haven't understood a thing. Here, for example, she is talking about cows and I know what a cow is. The word is very similar to the Swedish "ko." So, what is that "ard" at the end of "ko" as in *coward*? Is "ard" maybe another way of saying "are?" And what is "death" doing in that sentence? I wonder if the cows know that they are going to die. All this slaughter of cows is terrible. Why can't we just be vegetarian? Who wants to eat a cow anyway?

Miss Anderson asks Steve Netter to read the passage again. I know Steve. He sometimes sits at my lunch table and he is also enrolled in my Radio Announcing class. He is a good reader; not as wonderful as Miss Anderson, of course, but his voice sounds deep, determined, and proud. I have just started to get used to the boys' voices. I wonder what the word "valiant" means. I wonder if I can just sneak a quick peek into my Swedish/English Lexicon.

Miss Anderson asks the class to read the whole passage aloud together, and so together the class reads it once, and once again:

> *"Cowards die many times before their deaths.*
> *The valiant never taste of death but once.*
> *Of all the wonders that I yet have heard,*
> *It seems to me most strange that men should fear,*
> *Seeing that death, a necessary end,*
> *Will come when it will come."*

It sounds fine coming out from everyone like a singing chorus; like a slow wind over the ocean. The first two times, I just listen, but on the third time around, I read, too. I taste each word on my tongue as I let it loose and it flows from my lips together with all these English words that now hover around the room. So now I am part of the chorus. The words bounce about like helium-filled balloons. I can be together with everyone. My words float out with all these other English words. I am part of the English-speaking world. I belong. Comfort settles around me like a warming quilt.

Miss Anderson smiles. "Can anyone tell me in simple English just what Shakespeare is trying to say in that passage?"

Hands fly up and I am amazed. So, the passage is not in "simple English." Shakespeare was a great English writer. What kind of English did he write?

The golden-haired Amy gets to explain. Amy was voted "friendliest" in the sophomore class. She wears cashmere sweaters —cardigan over pullover in light blue. She speaks in a soft slur. I have to bend forward to really listen, and I am most anxious to get her explanation. "Well," Amy begins.

I wonder why all the students seem to do this. Why do they all say, "well," before they say anything else?

"Well," she says, "Shakespeare means that there is no use in always being scared of dying. Death, you know, will happen anyway, to everyone, some day. So, you know, what's the use of being scared all the time—many times; you might as well be brave. The brave people—the valiant—are not scared of death all the time. They only die once—the one time when, you know, their time comes to die."

I wonder about the "you know," that seems to crop into everything people say. They sprinkle it throughout every conversation. Shouldn't they be saying "I know?" I don't know anything. *Jag vet ingenting. Jag förstår ingenting.*[1]

"Nicely done, Amy," Miss Andersen bestows a benevolent smile and I hope that, someday, one will come my way. I understand the passage now, but I still wonder what happened to the cows.

Two and a half years later, I graduate from Bosse High School to head for Indiana State Teachers College in Terre Haute. I want to become a teacher. I want to be like Miss Andersen or the wonderful Mrs. Erskine, who taught me Plane Geometry, or the incredible Miss Cupp, Lenore Cupp, who taught me speech and drama, and chose me to play Henrietta, in *The Barretts of Wimpole*

Street, even though I could barely fake an American accent, much less a British one.

Dean Long helps me to obtain a scholarship. That money together with my part-time jobs should get me through college. Aunt Dora and Uncle Ben start me off with a loan of $200.00. So, I am going to make it, after all. They tell me that I speak with a Hoosier Accent. Ah! The lovely Hoosier accent. So now, I am a Hoosier. Who would have thought?

I am chosen to be one of the commencement speakers and I feel on top of the world. The principal introduces me with, "Natalie came to us two and half years ago. She didn't know a word of English, and we thought that she was a very quiet girl. Now we simply can't shut her up, so we are letting her do a student commencement talk. Enjoy!"

I speak fervently about "The American Dream", the possibilities offered to all, the beauty of democracy, and the unbound future that awaits us all. I have come to bloom in a garden of over-watered clichés, but I don't know this. I am a bit nervous, but I overcome my fears and speak with confidence and pride. Thank goodness, I am no coward!

AMBJ

I am 22 years old and a first-year teacher. Some of my students are seventeen-year-olds. I wear nylon stockings and very high-heeled pumps to distinguish myself from the bobby socks/Oxfords wearing students. I spend my free time making lesson plans and reading student papers.

The job is much harder than I had ever imagined it would be. Still, I remember the year as one in which I am enormously happy. Finally, I am an adult. I am making a grown-up salary. I am paying my own rent and buying my own food.

Finally, I don't have to be grateful to anyone. I am no one's unwanted child. I hadn't perhaps realized until then how heavy the burden of perpetual gratitude could be, but I certainly feel the relief from it. Walking to school in the mornings, on those high-heeled shoes, professionally dressed with pearls and earrings in place, I am encased in a bubble of contentment. A neighbor who watches me later confides that she had often asked herself, "What on earth makes that girl so happy?"

And, until loneliness hits and emptiness descends on me, I am indeed supremely happy. In truth, it's "fake it till you make it" in a big way. I am not yet a US citizen. I have spoken English for only five years, and here I am teaching Shakespeare to native born American youngsters, who call me Miss Boksenberg and seem to accept my status and my make-believe know-how.

As a teacher, I soon discover that asking the kind of questions to which I myself have no answer are the ones that bring about the most attention-grabbing lessons.

"Why doesn't Hamlet talk about the joys of life in *To be, or not to be?*" I ask. "What does Richard Cory, who is 'a gentleman from sole to crown,' in the poem by Edwin Arlington Robinson really look like? What does 'being a gentleman' mean? What do you have to do to be a gentleman? How does Richard Cory dress? Where does he live? Is there a Mrs. Cory? Does Richard own a dog? Why does Brutus betray Caesar? I don't know what the 'salesman' is selling in *The Death of ???*, do you?"

I let the students talk in pairs and in groups. Being a stage manager, I find easier than being the star of the show. And the stage-managing does create much more interesting lessons.

This is also the year I finally stop missing my parents, mamusia and tatus. I had always carried on long internal conversations with them first in Polish and later in Swedish, which, of course, they could not understand. Now occasionally, I turn to them in English, which has become my new "first language." But these days I turn to them less with longing and more with pride and joy. My sense is that I have done exactly what they would have wanted me to do.

"How should I dress for an interview?" I had asked them. "How should I behave towards the aunt and uncle in Evansville? How can I get all my work done without staying up half of the night? What is the best way to make cabbage soup? How do I make my apartment homey? Do I keep this particular friendship going? Do I tell this person how I really feel? What on earth is to become of me? Am I doing the right thing here?"

My two parents, dead in the furnaces of Treblinka, had more of less continued to lead me home. Somehow, it seems even more artificial to "speak" to them in English. American English seems so far removed, and Polish, my original first language, is steadily atrophying, as, sadly too, is my beloved Swedish. Anyway, I am an adult now. I can take care of myself. Perhaps I needn't talk with my parents so much. Perhaps they are as relieved as I am to be let go.

Then, with little warning, loneliness sneaks up on me. I watch the couples holding hands. I look at families sharing a meal. I long for a human touch, another voice at night, someone to rejoice with, and someone to cry with. At first, the loneliness is just a subtle whispering unease, but then it grows into a hovering monster, a weight of lead, a block of ice that refuses to melt. Weekends are the worst. What has it all been about? What is the point of life anyway? So, I am independent now. I no longer have to bear the burden of gratitude. But is that all there is to it?

Unexpectedly, I now understand why so many of my classmates at Indiana State Teachers' College in Terre Haute finished their senior year pregnant. *Didn't they know anything about birth control?* I had often wondered.

But now, after graduation, as I look around from my prideful professional outpost, I notice that there are no eligible men in the social picture. It seems that all the boys have been taken or *caught* as the saying then went. Had they perhaps all wanted to be caught? Were all my classmates so much smarter than I had ever been? Had they all made sure that they would not leave college to face the world alone? How could I have been so clueless?

This is, after all, the time when both the MRS and "Ph.T." (Putting Hubby Through) degrees are part of the cultural lingo, and I recall what one of my classmates had told me, quoting her mother: "You just get yourself a husband. That's what you do in college. That's the main thing. Once you have a husband, everything else will fall into place."

I remember thinking that my classmate's mother was delusional. Didn't she realize that getting a career was the thing that really mattered? Didn't she know that, first of all, one had to be independent? Now, suddenly, I question my own reasoning. Things in America are obviously different. How stupid of me not to have noticed that!

O.K. I would have to see what could be done. At the bottom of my bathroom mirror, I write A.M.B.J. (A man by June), and I begin to work on the project. I get a job teaching Sunday school at the Reform Temple in Sands Point. People start talking to me. It seems that everyone has a cousin, a son, or an uncle. "Would I like to meet?"

"Yes, thank you, I would."

And that starts a period of intense dating. I have to admit that I do not have an easy time with this quaint American way of courtship in the 50s. Here is how it works: You meet someone; you shake hands and say "Hello." He opens the car door for you, and drives you to a movie, or maybe out to dinner (so, a car seems to be a requirement of the arrangement). You make vacuous conversation. You ask about his job or his studies or his future plans. You listen tensely for some aspect of what he said that can be embellished. Does he participate in sports? What is his political outlook? Which movies does he like? The glossy magazines had instructed to make him talk, and, above all, to "laugh at his jokes." But they had also warned to look for "someone with a future." At the end of the date, he walks you to your door, and then you are expected to participate in the obligatory good night kiss. Some, of course, expect a great deal more, but those I have no trouble dealing with. The wet kiss part is tame enough, but I find it arriving far too early for physical intimacy of any kind. I have, after all, just met this guy a couple of hours ago, and now I am supposed to kiss him? I hate that part. The kisses are soggy, sticky, clammy, and unpleasant, and that is certainly as far as I go.

Hey, I was a literature major. I had read Theodore Dreiser's *American Tragedy*, not to speak of Herman Wouk's *Marjorie Morning Star*. I know that a nice Jewish girl remains a virgin and "saves herself" for her one-and-only true intended. But how and where to find him?

Anxiously, I scour the magazines that explain all that. Realizing how lagging I am in these cultural issues, I carefully study every relevant magazine from *Seventeen* to *Glamour* as well other socially minded publications that cater to the young professional woman, and I valiantly try to follow their recommendations: I join an amateur actors' group, I join Young Democrats, I take some graduate courses at Columbia University, anything to meet people.

"Circulate, circulate, circulate," is the magazine mantra. But how am I supposed to do all that and get my students' papers checked and my lesson plans in order? Well, it just has to be done. There is the A.M.B.J glaring at me from my bathroom mirror each morning, and I keep at it.

And then, uncannily, my work pays off, just like that, without warning. Nathaniel Hess, Nat, my future father-in-law, is one of the founders of that very upscale reform congregation in Sands Point, where I get a job teaching Sunday School. He is a bigwig, a tall impressive man, married to the beautiful Marjorie, who had been an opera singer in her younger years, and who now leads the temple choir. Nat had actually been the one who hired me for the Sunday School teaching job, but since then, he had never even glanced my way, so that I am a bit surprised, when one morning during break, he approaches me. His style is appealingly direct. "Well, young lady," he says. "I think that you are good-looking enough to be introduced to my son. Are you interested?"

Needless to say, I am. These days, I never say "no" to such things. It is, after all, already March. June isn't that far down the road. And this is how I meet John.

John is the tall Jewish nerd that I had always dreamed about, but never really expected to find. We do not go to the movies. He does not open the car door for me. He does not kiss me goodnight until much later. We have one awkward dinner at a French restaurant, but then we keep going to New York and walking a lot.

He knows the subway system like palm of his hand, and he buys me a Hershey bar from a vending machine, and he takes me to visit his elementary school, City and Country, in Greenwich Village, where we sneak down to the basement and find his scholastic record in a long-neglected filing cabinet. We visit the UN and are amazed at the seeming efficiency and cooperation there.

Remember, we are still very young and very hopeful about the world. We sit around in libraries, where I mark papers and he studies physics. He tells me sadly that he has just flunked the oral part of his physics test, and so had to give up the Ph.D. program he had been hoping to participate in, but he was going to try for it again.

We are walking in Central Park holding hands when he tells me that his parents are divorced. This takes me by surprise. I had wondered why I felt so comfortable with him. I thought that he was Nat's and Marjorie's son, and somehow my war-orphan self could not envision me as accepted or feeling that I belonged in that family. But with the news of the divorce, a completely different family story emerges.

"I was the baby, who was supposed to cement the marriage, but I obviously did not succeed at the job," he explains. Both parents remarried, and he was not at home in either family. He is happy to have grown up and not have to spend much time with either group.

My God, my mind delights. *He is an orphan just like I am.*

And that thought is the serious turning point in our relationship. Now we talk about loneliness, about personal beliefs, about the shape of families, and about our sense of what the future might bring. We hold hands a lot, and we talk endlessly. I tell him that I have applied for a scholarship to study in France, but that I am seriously considering going to live in Israel. He tells me that he would prefer France.

I explain that it isn't so simple. "If after two thousand years of yearning, the Jews are finally back in their home, and if this miracle is happening in our lifetime, doesn't that imply the obligation of going there to live?"

He smiles with vague understanding, but he is not convinced.

And that first kiss, when it finally comes, melts the lead and dissolves the ice, and I want many repetitions. This is my guy. Together neither one of us is an orphan. We are a couple. We are going to be a family. We finally both belong.

We are in my small apartment in the process of eating a hastily prepared lunch, when the telephone rings, and John answers.

"Hello Marjorie," I hear him say. "I am just fine, thank you. Just fine. How are you?" There is a slight silence, and then I hear John clearing his throat. "Yes," he says, "there actually is something new, as a matter of fact. The new thing is that I am getting married."

I hear him say it. So naturally, so easily and so fluently he just says it. And instinctively I know that this is the only "proposal" I will ever get.

Afterwards things just proceed.

"You know, you are not as good looking as I thought you were," his father one day remarks.

"Well, too bad," I tell him. "You should have noticed that sooner. It's too late now. We are in love."

We are married in the rabbi's study on June 20, 1958. It is a very simple wedding, but it turns into a beautiful marriage.

It lasts 53 years and produces three remarkable daughters and six outstanding grandchildren, and until he leaves this world, we endlessly talk and talk, and kiss a great deal, as well.

THE HESS DRESS

After John leaves for his new job in Boston, the Hesses invite me to join them for Friday night services. They are founding members of the Sands Point Jewish Reform congregation adjacent to the village of Port Washington where I had found my first teaching job, at the Paul D. Schreiber High School. I had briefly visited the Hess home once together with John, so I know that all the homes in Sands Point could easily qualify for the *Better Homes and Gardens* cover page, but even in the midst of such an exclusive group, the Hess house is, as I am frequently told, "something very special."

Marjorie, John's stepmother, leads the temple choir. She is known in the community as a Hebrew scholar and a stern interviewer of all prospective rabbis.

"She would drive us all crazy," one well-known rabbi tells me many years later. "She is, after all, kind of a star, the daughter of the great Rabbi Levy of Chicago. As a child, she spent a year in Israel. She speaks Hebrew fluently, and let's face it, she still is drop-dead gorgeous and still can be very demanding. You definitely have to please Marjorie Hess if you want to become a Reform rabbi in the Sands Point Congregation."

Nathaniel Hess (Nat) is a major contributor and organizer in the congregation. The Hess home (I always thought of it as the Hess mansion) features sunken living spaces, roomy bedrooms and multiple bathrooms. The gardens surrounding the house are not simply beautiful and well tended, which indeed they are, but, for their time, they are also highly original.

Nat is truly a landscape artist. The gardens he creates and tends have the feel of an imagined English meadow stylized in Japanese fashion. Every carefully tended blade of grass seems naturally windblown. Colors of flowers mesh seamlessly with moss and stones to create a sense of peaceful fusion. An occasional terrace adds to a sense of natural flow. Here and there multi-colored African Daisies lean into purely pink begonia. Annuals frame perennials, and sturdy artichoke edges in on lady-like Aster. The Hess garden at Sands Point has won many prizes and is considered one of the show places of the community.

When the Hesses invite me to join them at Friday night services, I feel as if I had been summoned by Queen Elizabeth to Buckingham Palace. Standing together with them in the synagogue would, in a way, serve as my official and public entry into the family. For some moments, I allow myself to wonder how I, the newly minted schoolteacher, can possibly ever fit into such a fold. By this time, I also know that John has never felt part of this particular framework.

"Growing up, I hated this whole show," he tells me. "Yes, I gave the required smile when pictures were taken, pretending that we were just one happy family. I knew quite well that I was just in everyone's way. Not that their four kids were visions of contentment either. Lots of things were happening behind the Hess glory and the beautiful gardens."

Well, come what may. I had to play my part well.

On my way home from school, I stop at the very expensive dress boutique on Main Street in Port Washington. I have often longingly gazed at this particular store's display window, but it is not a place I had ever thought of frequenting. On a beginning teacher's salary, it is way out of my budgetary bounds. But this time it has to be done. I have to be appropriately dressed for a social occasion with the Hesses. I have to be a worthy future-daughter-in-law.

The minute I enter the store, ineptness clings to me like a rain-soaked wool sweater. The perfume of something floral and French subdues my senses. Several overstuffed chairs imply that this is a temple of exclusive leisure to which I am warmly welcomed, but where I will clearly suffer indignities if I am not prepared to pay the price for the distinctiveness it affords. Promptly, I give up all thought of self-restraint and put myself in the hands of the concerned and judicious sales lady.

"That dress really suits you," she says. "And you, my dear, are just right for it. You and that dress, spell class, darling. Real class!"

Well, this lady certainly knows her job. "Class" is just the word I want to hear right now! Her approval is essential and I buy the dress for one half of June's salary. The dress is made of pure white linen. The sleeves are three-quarter-length. The dress has a high collar, which somehow makes it feel Victorian, and appeals to my sense of romanticism. Small pearl buttons accentuate the sides of the sleeves. The skirt hugs my hips and flares at the knees.

The minute I get home I pull it out of the bag and try it on in front of my full-length bathroom mirror. Here at home, I really don't like it so much, but in defense of what has obviously been character weakness, I decide that it looks sophisticated and is appropriate for the evening's event. For a brief few minutes, I consider adding a black shawl as a contrasting wrap, but I reject the idea. This dress has to be seen alone in its full glory.

As it happens, this turns out to be a very bad decision.

There is a lot of standing up and sitting down during a Friday night Jewish Reform service. At a crucial moment, I feel a delicate touch on my shoulder, and I hear the lady in back of me gently whispering, "My dear, I think you should know that the back of your skirt is stained."

I live through the remainder of the service in a state of paralyzing mortification. How could I have been such an idiot? Why of all colors had I chosen pure white? Why, on earth, hadn't I added the black shawl? How am I going to face the world now? Shame and agony wash over me. Why isn't there a trap door that will open up to swallow me? How will I get up... get out? Marjorie will be in back of me as we walk out. She will, of course, notice. What am I going to say? What should I do? How could I have been so stupid? *Please, Dear Lord, just get me out of here!*

As it turns out, I need not have worried. Marjorie, bless her heart, also heard the whisper. She offers her shawl as cover, and she insists that I return home with them.

The Hess's splendid living room is furnished in angular blond wood, accentuated by carefully structured flower arrangements that consist mostly of South African Protea backed by complementary greens. This, of course is long before every office throughout the world has adopted the style then known as Danish Modern. I had never really seen it so elegantly displayed, and I am wildly impressed.

I will never forget the generosity of spirit offered me by the Hesses during that visit. They treat me with friendliness and respect. They clearly see me as qualified to become a family member. They certainly could have taken me straight home, or shown disapproval over my unseemly exposure. Instead, they offer sympathy and affability. In spite of John's clear distaste of anything attached to either one of his families, I always felt gratitude and affinity for the Hess side, which seemed to accept me in an openhearted and egalitarian manner. Throughout our marriage, Marjorie remained an ideally supportive and friendly mother-in-law. Of course, she was not John's mother—and that, no doubt, made it easier.

During this particular visit to the Hess house, Marjorie offers sympathy, a trip to the bathroom, a pair of slacks, and a bag for my now discolored dress. The eternal "curse" makes us "girls together."

Marjorie shows me family pictures. There is nine-year-old John together with the four Hess siblings in front of the Thanksgiving turkey. There is a series of these from age nine to about age fourteen and then no more. In each picture John looks miserable— not even a single artificial smile. His description to me had been accurate. He didn't belong with the Hess siblings, and he didn't belong with the Merton siblings, on his mother's side, either. In both families, he always saw himself as the outcast, posing as a family member.

I didn't think about it then, but even though I was certainly awed with the glory of it all, I did somehow grasp that John, in these surroundings, had been just as much of a hanging-on orphan as I had been in my various unreal family constructs.

"Well, the performance is over," John once explained to me. "By the time I got to high school, I had pretty much decided not to participate in the loving-family pretense. By then, I understood that I was the baby my parents had produced to keep a bad marriage together. It obviously didn't work. I just wasn't up to the job. Well, too bad! At any rate, I am no longer in any mood to do the 'perfect family' stuff for their picture parades. So, please don't feel that you have to take on that job."

I believe that this visit to the Hess house gave me a sense that the family John and I would create could not be built on the shaky foundations of our previous experiences. It would have to be a unique creation of our own.

Marjorie shows an album featuring her much younger self as a beautiful opera singer. Her beauty stuns me, and like a total fool, I endlessly repeat, "Oh Marjorie you were uncanny! What an amazing beauty you were."

Somehow, I feel that I have displeased her.

Looking back at this from my present lofty age, I can only be amazed at my youthful inanity. Of course, she wants me to point out how absolutely gorgeous she still is—and indeed she is that! Her heart-shaped face surrounded by soft black curls bears resemblance to Elizabeth Taylor's. Her figure has exactly the right proportion of fullness so treasured in the 1950s, but being the 22-year-old dope that I was at the time, I still did not understand such things—well, I would certainly learn.

From pictures we move to greater intimacy.

"Would you like to see some old family letters? They might help you to understand Johnny better."

What a question. Of course I would.

John's mother, Felice, begging her former husband for financial support had, 20 years earlier, written these now yellowed letters that Marjorie shows me. Felice, who at the time, lived in Vienna with her second husband, an Austrian ski instructor, seemed to be in constant financial need:

She needs funds for John's nursery school.

She needs money for domestic help.

She needs money for taking John to the beach.

She needs money to buy summer outfits for John.

The letters embarrass me, and I wonder why Marjorie decided to share them. Presumably, it is her attempt to let me into parts of my future husband's life. At the time, I feel terribly sorry for Felice in her beggarly position. I also somehow feel intensely disloyal to John. Should I be exposed to this version of Felice, who was such a proud woman? I wonder if the money was supplied and think about how terrible it must feel to be so reliant on male support.

The year is 1958—child support has not yet become established practice. I am a beginning teacher with a small salary, but at this moment I remind myself of my professional status and my personal independence, and I promise myself that I will never place myself in a state of such total dependency—never! I look up from reading the letters and become, once more, aware of the luxurious surroundings of the Hess décor, but at this moment this lavish interior seems to mock me. What use is all this, if it is only power derived by way of graciousness from the male provider with power that can be removed at his pleasure?

John's mother, Felice Merton, like his father at this time, also lives the upscale life of Long Island—if not quite up to the Hess style, the Merton home nevertheless displays similar economic territory. I know Felice, now, in her third marriage, as a gracious hostess at home within her upper-middle-class ambiance.

Yet here was her younger self begging for money—even stretching her stories of need. How very humiliating it all seems to me. I re-read the letters, promising myself that I will never allow this to happen to me. No diamond ring on my finger would be worth such a state of financial supplication.

That evening, Nat drives me home, and I try desperately and unsuccessfully to make polite conversation.

"When are you going to quit your job and join Johnny in Boston?" Nat asks.

"First, I have to finish the school year, and find a new job in Boston," I promptly tell him, even though up to this moment I have not structured any such plans.

In my small apartment, I relish the "back home" feeling. This one room apartment is my place. I paid the rent. I could afford it. I take my newly bought dress out from the bag that Marjorie had given me, and I spend a long moment staring at the red, now encrusted blood stain. Clearly, this stain exposes my vulnerability, but it also offers me a curious warning of how quickly and unpredictably life can be discolored and how all human relationships and endeavors are constantly challenged.

That evening in a fit of emotional anguish, I throw away the dress. I never tell John about the evening. I also continue to work until age 75.

SPUTNIK AND SHAKESPEARE

The year is 1957. I am 22 years old, and a first-year teacher at Paul D. Schreiber High School in Port Washington, New York. Amazingly, I am on my own and doing just fine. I become an American citizen in Mineola, and the kids in my seventh period class made me a cake covered by miniature American flags. And then, I start pretending to be the genuine American article. After all, I graduated as English major and I am teaching *Julius Caesar* by William Shakespeare.

Then suddenly, October 4th, 1957, there is Sputnik, and everything changes. Wonder and amazement capture the world. Human beings have actually ventured into outer space. Where will this lead? Which fantasy is next? Is it actually true that we eventually do all the things that we have previously only imagined? This is a serious slap in America's face. There is mile-high American dismay! There is a mile-high American missile gap! America was supposed to do this first. America was supposed to be number one in the space race.

And I wonder if there is still room for Shakespeare. Nobody knows. Who cares for Shakespeare, when Sputnik is dancing around the moon? Soviet propaganda rings with the pride of achievement. Urgency propels science and math education in the developed world. Rockets are built in Middle American basements, and here in Port Washington, Long Island at Paul D. Schreiber High School, the superintendent of schools, Dr. Yerek, calls an emergency meeting of all school staff.

"Little Ivan is sending ships to outer space!" he thunders. "But our little Johnny can't read!" He is a short man and his fury is evident.

I feel guilty. Somehow some of his annoyance falls on me in a very personal way. Dr. Yerek pauses and lets out a significant breath. He waits, and we wait with him. We are all sad together. The silence is heavy with regret and retribution.

Dr. Yerek's voice reemerges. He pleads and scolds. He admonishes and reprimands. "We must change," he says. "Change we must! It is up to you, you educators, you who face our children every day to make those changes." His long sober gaze holds us. "It is our essential duty to change things. Our children have been coddled. I have checked on their homework assignments—much too light, much too easy. Make them work! Make them struggle! Make them think. Make them compete with those clever Russian children. Educate them! That's your job! Let's face it, if we don't educate our children, the Russians are going to conquer the moon."

Horrified by such a possibility and burdened by a weighty commission, I return to class and make a crucial decision: my poor sophomores will have to memorize large sections of Mark Anthony's speech from *Julius Caesar*. Some of my students will probably show off by memorizing the speech in its entirety. And I stick to my resolution by showing through good example.

The entire project causes all of us enormous pain, but I am sure that my students, who, no doubt, and as a result of these efforts, have turned into appreciative readers and perhaps even into nuclear engineers. Perhaps they are grateful to me until this very day. At any rate, come what may, at the moment, I feel that I have fulfilled my patriotic duty just as Dr. Yerek has urged me to do. And later, when President Kennedy announces that America would within the decade transport a man to the moon, my heart swells with pride. Once America has settled that cosmic sphere, I am sure that Shakespeare will be studied there.

ARE WE THERE YET?

In 1963, I am pregnant with my second child. Six months later, it turns out to be my daughter, Deborah, but, of course, I don't know that yet. This is before the time of the all-knowing ultrasound.

1963 is also the year the feminist movement produces its first bud with the publication of Betty Friedan's *Feminine Mystique*, which speedily hits the best-seller list and reframes the role of "homemaker," a title that most of us still hold in high esteem. The great majority of us are preparing and even pining for the *MRS degree* and are quite willing to struggle toward the *Ph.T. (Putting Hubby Through)*. Such achievements would give us the ultimate reward of children, washer and dryer humming, and the waft of apple pie drifting from our sparkling kitchens—visions that immediately follow the white-wedding-dress-fantasy of our lives.

Once we have found a husband, we are told, everything else will fall into place, provided, of course, that we have been clever enough to "catch someone with a future." Teaching is one of the three "honorable" professions we can approach; the other two being nursing or secretarial work. We earn these professional qualifications as a "just in case... you never know" policy.

Those of us who become teachers invariably work under male supervision, for the principal is always a he, but on the whole, we feel good about things. After all, we have long ago outgrown the one-room schoolmarms, who were told to place their slips and other "unmentionables" inside pillowcases before hanging them out on clotheslines to publicly dry.

So, here is a personal case in point—a real story of the social capital and the way things were.

That winter I have just started "to show." "To show" is the delicate terminology used to describe the moment in which tummy expansion during one's "fragile condition" shows evidence of life to come. This is also the moment when I know that I must notify my principal, and make a subtle, yet graceful exit from professional endeavors.

One is not allowed to teach in the public school system once the crucial "it" starts *to show*. An unwritten, but clearly understood part of the contract of the female life cycle in education, yes, my dear young friends, it's true. I know that it's hard for you to believe; you who teach until the last second, you, whose young students gently rub your tummy and inquire whether the baby is kicking. In 1963, however, it is so. I know the rules. I will not be returning after Christmas vacation. And it was called CHRISTMAS vacation in those days—not winter break— not holiday vacation. We also start the day by reading three verses from the Bible (King James version, of course) in homeroom.

But back to my story; nobody seems to mind. At least nobody much dares to question the situation or even consider questioning it.

In the Boston suburbs of 1963, I have two jobs. I am teaching English in high school in one suburb and, while in a second community, I also teach some evening courses for adults. The adults are French Canadians, and I am teaching English (English as a Second Language, ESL, as it will later be described). The French

Canadians are older folks. I am 27, and some of my students could easily be my parents, others possibly even my grandparents.

I am well aware of the "quit as soon as you show" rule, but I assume that it is designated for the youngsters I teach during the day. They, of course, under no circumstances, should suspect me of naughty bedtime activity in my private life. After all, I am an educator. I duly notify the principal of the day school of my delicate predicament, and receive a beatific farewell with the understanding that I will not be returning to my professional status, as I now must assume, "my real function in life" (direct quote). I also wrongly assume that the "quit as soon as you show" rule does not apply in the case of my adult evening learners, since, delicacy or no delicacy, they should be aware of how these things work, and here is how I learn about my mistaken assumption.

It is Monday evening, and I emerge from my class for the customary break. Mr. Howard (not his real name), the principal of the evening school, stands at the classroom door. He has clearly been waiting for me. He is a rather stout man, somewhere in his late 50s. He wears a double-breasted brown suit. His loosened tie is bright red and finds echo in the high color of his face. His grayish hair, which is usually neatly pasted down to cover the right front bit of baldness appears mussed and disarranged. I sense a state of discomfort, perhaps even agitation about the man, as his crooked finger repeatedly indicates that I should follow him into his office.

Once we are both there, he assumes a protected position behind his desk, as I humbly stand before him. He makes no indication that implies seating for either one of us. He bends down to fumble with scattered papers, and then clears his throat a number of times. I stand before him completely befuddled. Something is clearly wrong here. But, what?

My classes have been going well. My students treat me with growing affection. I frequently build vocabulary contents on the homemade pastries that appear on my desk. These are highly motivated students and their language learning grows by leaps and bounds. We can read *Time* magazine and discuss current issues with greater and greater proficiency as well as political acuity. I must say that I am rather proud of the progress we have made, but it is amply clear to me that at this point I am definitely not in line for commendation or accolade.

Mr. Howard glances in my direction and then looks down again. His throat clearing sounds grow more insistent, and this time he deigns me an exploratory gaze. "Mrs. Hess," he finally enunciates with strong emphasis on those last two ss's, "Mrs. Hess, I want to tell you that I was stopped by the custodian tonight and he said to me..." and here Mr. Howard returns to the ferocious clearing of his throat. He produces a handkerchief from his pocket and spends some time touching up his nose. He looks down again and up again, but it is a look that desperately attempts not to see me. For some reason he wants to avoid looking at me. His embarrassment overflows and my lack of ease joins his. Whatever have I done?

"Ah, as I said," Mr. Howard continues. "As I previously mentioned, Mr. Block, the custodian, you know, stopped me in the hallway this evening, and he said to me. Well, he said to me, hmmm... hmmm... Well, he asked me. He said..." and here Mr. Howard's voice becomes quite shrill. He looks at me once more and now there is some kind of recognition in his face as his breath quickens and he pours it all out, "Mr. Block asked me, 'Did you know... well...did you know that Mrs. Hess is carrying... that she's carrying a bundle?' That's what the custodian said to me, you know."

There is finally a sense of great release here in poor Mr. Howard's voice as he again quite clearly announces, "Did you notice, I say, did you notice that Mrs. Hess is really carrying a BUNDLE?"

A light switches on in my muddled head, "Yes, I am pregnant," I say.

There ensues a rather friendly silence. The discomfiture has suddenly melted away.

"Do you mean that I should have quit as soon as it showed?" I inquire.

Mr. Howard shakes his head in wonder. He seems ever so much more relaxed, ever so relieved. The poor man. He might have had to explain it all to me. But thank heaven, he has been able to make his point to this incredibly dense woman.

"But they are adults," I say. "They are grown-ups, so I thought. Well, it never occurred to me that. Honestly."

"Yes," Mr. Howard agrees, and now his smile is very friendly. "They are indeed. But you see we are part of the school system, and we must obey those rules. And you will be very busy soon I expect. Won't you?"

"Yes," I expected I would be. Fortunately, my husband, who was still a graduate student, had his scholarship and some extra funds, and after an intensive search I find another evening job at Boston University, where in the more open academic environment "the rule" no longer applies. So, 1963 is a year of transition. The Civil Rights Movement is also going strong. We are all in transit.

PART 4
LIFE IN ISRAEL

THE SIX-DAY WAR

"Well, sweetheart. Of course you are worried," *Dodah*[1] Marta says. She passes a hand through her backswept gray hair and heaves her ample bosom into a worldly sigh of competent assurance. "It is, after all, your first war here," she tells me. She is using her decisive know-it-all nursery-school-teacher voice, the tone she applies when addressing concerned but mildly annoying parents.

The timbre is supposed to exude professionally framed comfort —the voice of firmly grounded, established and time-honored maturity, but for me this particular inflection has always and invariably signaled Israeli arrogance—the just barely covered-over tolerance for the dumb American, the naive American which is what I seem to have become in this new self-imposed identity. "You take care of your home, *Motek* (sweetie), and you let *Zahal* (the Israeli Defense Forces, IDF) worry about national security," Dodah Marta concludes. The condescension is clearly there. I am on my way home.

It's 1967 and we have lived in Israel for two and a half years. Our first two years were in Rechovot. Only the last half-year has been spent in Jerusalem.

On Sunday[2], June 4, I clutch Debby's little hand, and push the baby carriage where Tammy peacefully sleeps. Dodah Marta's barely veiled condescension penetrates and settles in. We move up the hill on *Korey Hadorot* Street, our street. Debby chatters about a new girlfriend. "Can we invite Sarah to play tomorrow, mommy?"

"Good idea! We'll do that."

"But mom, she is going to be MY girlfriend—MINE, not Becky's. Becky always takes my girlfriends away! Are you listening, mom?"

No I am not. I ought to be, but I am not. My stomach churns and my heart pounds, and in addition, my pride hurts. I was clearly not going to get any prizes for staying put, while every other American I knew had already flown the coop, but, here in Talpiot there were no other Americans, and, for that matter, was I really an American?

Well, John certainly was. Had we really considered our decision with the seriousness that it demanded? Not really. On May 14, just three weeks earlier, President Nasser of Egypt had mobilized thousands of troops in and around the Suez Canal. On May 22, Egypt had closed the straits of Tiran to Israeli shipping—a step that clearly was an act of war. On May 31, Egypt declared that the goal was "to wipe Israel off the map." The Six-Day war had begun!

We do not have a television set. Israeli television does not begin broadcasting until 1968. John listens to BBC. I read *Time Magazine*—my link to the USA. In the previous week's issue General de Gaulle, had declared his staunch belief that the stiff-necked Jews would soon be a wandering people again. And then there were those demanding letters from Felice telling us in so many words how irresponsible we were to endanger our children. Was she right? Were we crazy?

My only answer was that this was a Jewish country and these were Jewish children. No other child on the block was leaving. Should mine be able to leave simply because they had American passports? John and I had come on Aliyah[3] two years earlier. We had made the commitment. I had always been a Zionist, and it had taken me some six years, with great help from Leon Uris's best-selling novel, *Exodus,* to convince John that he too was one.

It seemed to me that if this incredible miracle of Jewish return to the once promised and always longed for homeland had actually materialized and done so in our own lifetimes then we were surely obliged to live to be part of the marvel. If, after all those centuries of longing, after all those centuries of "next year in Jerusalem" had actually bloomed into physical reality, why then we certainly had the obligation to partake in it and most importantly to make our children part of it.

What was also true for me was the worry that with my own meager Jewish education and with John's total lack of such, we would never be able to bring up Jewish children in America. And there was no question in my mind that my existential duty demanded that I bring Jewish children to the world. But at this particular juncture, dream and reality were seriously colliding. Suppose anything happened to my living, breathing, beloved children. Would I ever be able to forgive myself? Well, of course, nothing was going to happen. There really wasn't going to be a war. Was there? My stomach churns with fear and anxiety.

Debby is pulling on my sweater. "Can I have an *Artic* (popsicle), mommy?"

We stop at Levin's grocery store. It's just a hole in the wall, but he has everything from ice cream to Indian noodles, and he knows us well. We are good customers. We don't need cash or credit card. He keeps a list and we pay once a month.

We are renting an old Talpiot House on 17 Korey Hadorot Street. It is only a few blocks away from the house of Shay Agnon, the later Nobel-prize laureate. But in spite of its famous resident, the neighborhood literally sags. The houses were built before anyone realized that in Talpiot ground was constantly moving.

As a result, all the floors of the old Talpiot houses are uneven.

125

Ours is no exception. Our dining table sits on a naturally raised slightly wavy platform above the living room area. Somehow, I find it charming. The neighborhood borders no man's land where, *Armon Hanatziv*, Government House—the former mansion of the British governor—is located. In this year of 1967, the United Nations observers reside in Government House. On the other side of Government house is the Kingdom of Jordan.

Across the street from our house in the lot that belongs to the Lazarus family, a huge crater has been dug out. A cannon has been placed in the hole where two men fiddle with the cannon. One is a very young soldier. His youthful face attests to a fairly recent high school graduation. The other fellow looks like a middle-aged reservist. Debby, still enjoying her sticky, dripping popsicle, wants to stop and look, so we cross over. Several other neighbors are there. Jimmy Lazarus, from South Africa, who is my friend, is there with his two small daughters—Orly and Talia. "Looks like a very sturdy cannon," he sagely declares.

"Looks old fashioned to me," says Tova Shapira from up the street, "I hope it works."

The young soldier down there in the hole seems to have the same concerns. He is clearly confused as to the workings of this particular mechanical monster. "I don't get it!" he tells his more experienced partner. "I will never be able to work this thing." Sweat is pouring down his baby features.

"You are just nervous," his older partner assures him. "Just think of it as your washing machine. Don't worry about what happens up there. You just push those buttons on your washing machine. Do the wash! You got a washing machine?"

"My mom does," the young one mumbles.

"Ever help out with the wash?" his buddy asks. This is followed by strained silence. "Well, I tell you what," the older one concludes, "tonight, when you get home, you do some wash for your mom. I know she will appreciate it."

Debby has finished her *Artic*. Tammy, in the carriage, is waking up. Becky and John will be home any time now. We cross the street for lunch, the main meal in Israel, and perhaps a nap. I had pounded and tenderized the schnitzels. The baked potatoes are in the oven, and a salad has been cut up. Between two and four in the afternoon, kids are not allowed to play outside—too much noise —*Schlaf Stunde*—Siesta time in Israel.

We eat lunch and the kids go down for a nap. I clear up lunch and John naps briefly, and then returns to work at the Hebrew University.

"Don't worry," he tells me as he gives me a casual hug and a perfunctory peck on the cheek. "We are safe here in Talpiot right on the border. King Husein will never start anything. He is smart enough to know that if he does, he is going to lose the old city."

Monday, June 5, starts out with the usual routine. The girls are up at 5:30. Tammy is up first and yells for "Bebby" and "Kacki" (Debby and Becky). Her two sisters leave their bunks to jump into her crib, where they manage to keep themselves entertained until I show up for diaper and dress detail. There is fresh bread from Levin's. John eats pancakes with honey. Becky likes sliced radishes. Debby prefers cucumbers. Tammy has just recently switched from breast to bottle and relishes the milk mixture. I am in love with the Israeli "Black Bread," and with difficulty as well as encouragement from the local Weight Watcher group, struggle mightily to limit myself to the heel—my very favorite section, especially with herring and onions.

The table on its wavy floor tips a bit, but John catches the honey jar before it hits the floor and prevents what would have certainly become a major sticky spill. He will drive our small Cortina station wagon to work and drop Debby off at Dodah Marta's Nursery School and Becky at the pre-kindergarten, a few blocks farther down the street. Tammy is happy in the playpen while I do dishes and straighten up. I move the playpen outside when I go out to hang the diapers on the line that stretches between two trees in our large and unkempt backyard.

With Tammy in her stroller, I head for Levin's. I need some fresh vegetables for the midday meal. I choose a beautiful head of lettuce, sorely tempted by four almost overripe tomatoes that talk to me in their irresistible redness and plump glory but they are expensive and I settle for cucumbers, peas, and a bunch of juicy carrots. There is milk, which comes in plastic bags, which will fit, into a special container made just for this purpose. The chicken waits in the fridge and has already been plucked, cleaned, and cut into portions. Mr. Levin places my purchases neatly in the lid of a carton next to my American, Boston-bought wallet. He arranges the carton, so that I can balance it on the handlebars of Tammy's stroller. Tammy and I are back home around 11:30.

The shelling starts just as I put the carton on the kitchen counter. I grab Tammy and dash for the shelter. Chavie Cahanne, my upstairs neighbor, who is Dodah Marta's daughter-in-law, is already there with her three-month old baby, Offer.

"Good thing we got this place cleaned out last week," she says. "I heard on the radio that the Jordanians have already taken Government House."

"Oh my God," I can hear my own voice tremble, "and I didn't even grab a knife from the kitchen."

"That's all right," Chavie assures me, "I have a gun." And she holds up a green plastic bag that presumably holds the required weapon.

We huddle together on one of the two benches available. The shelter is a small windowless room about six feet wide and seven feet long. It is located right under my kitchen and is accessed from the side alley next to the house. The entrance is only a few feet away from the street.

If we open the door we can just see our street, but now we have firmly closed the door, and the air in the shelter is heavy. Chavie's husband, Itshak, serves in the Jerusalem reservists.

My head spins and I feel my legs shaking. Tammy snuggles up. And there is the breast, still available for comfort, a soothing consolation for both mother and child. But then my thoughts start to fly wildly. An acrid mass of fear crunches my insides. John is at the Hebrew University. Surely there must be a shelter there. I know that Dodah Marta has a good one. And the kindergarten, which both Becky and Chavie's son Tahl attend, uses the shelter in a private home across the street.

Tammy is satisfied and makes good use of the limited floor space. There is a spare diaper in my pocket. Chavie is nursing. She holds Offer close and sings a lullaby. From the green bag of the promised gun, she pulls a surprising jar of olives. Tammy grabs one, and I have a hard time removing the choking hazard pit from her mouth.

We hear the shelling upstairs. Chavie and I with the babies between us cling to each other. Something is clearly hitting my kitchen. A whack and the unmistakable sound of glass breaking. Then there is absolute silence. Offer, between us, starts crying. The bag with the gun falls to the floor. We sit in silence. Speaking would bring out our worst fears.

In the late afternoon, Tammy falls asleep and I sneak out front to look at the street. Moving towards me in what appears to be slow motion—an elaborate dance of some kind—is John with three children, Becky and Debby both in red cardigans knitted by Aunt Dora in Evansville, and Tahl Cahanne in brown.

I know that I should turn back to tell Chavie that they are coming, but I am rooted to my spot and cannot budge. What am I waiting for? A piece of shrapnel to hit them; a bomb from the sky to destroy them? I want to shout, "Be careful!" But careful of what? No sound comes from my mouth.

John and the children are moving slowly, each step a balancing act of some sort. Somehow the realization reaches my brain. John must be watching that they don't step on all the electrical wiring that now is strewn all over the street. And then, suddenly it seems, they are with me and I hold them, and want to melt with them, disappear with them. I cannot let them go. John kisses me slowly.

His fingers trace the outline of my face. His eyes are tired and worried. The girls squeeze in between us. For a moment we are one solidly existing universe. For a moment, the sense of safety embraces us. We are together. For a moment, all is right with the world.

John spreads his coat on the floor. The children curl up on it and promptly go to sleep. Debby's thumb is firmly ensconced behind her lips. Becky's sleepy point finger is caught in the midst of its habitual hair-twirl. Tammy is on my shoulder. She too drops her head and is soon breathing the soft, sweeping breaths of contented baby slumber.

"The Jordanians have taken Government House," I tell John.

He is listening to *"Galey Zahal"* (the Israeli army station) on his portable radio. "We got it back," he tells me.

"No way," I say. "It's your lousy Hebrew. You must have misunderstood."

John hands the radio over to Chavie. Her face glows. She shakes her head and her curls bounce. She is clearly delighted. "John is right," she says. "Zahal just got it back. We won't need this gun after all."

I remember John's prediction yesterday. Was it really just yesterday?

"Well, I guess King Husein wasn't as smart as you thought he was," I tell John. He is amused and we tell Chavie about John's prediction.

"John is obviously smarter that that little king," she says. "He should have listened to John."

Chavie is worried about our friend, Ada Gorni, who is alone with two small children in the neighborhood of Arnona up the hill. Ada's house has no shelter. Her husband serves with Itshak Cahanne in the Jerusalem reserve unit.

"We have to bring Ada and her kids here," Chavie pleads.

John offers to look for Ada. I am terrified to see him go, but I realize that it must be done. After all, John is the only husband who has not yet been drafted.

"Please don't go," I beg. "Please, please don't leave me."

"I'll be back with Ada in 20 minutes," he assures me.

In normal time, that walk back and forth from Arnona would indeed take only about 20 minutes, but now there is still the intermittent sound of shelling and I am in a state of terror. "Please stay, honey," I beg.

But go, of course, he must and, of course, he does.

Time moves at watched teapot pace. The kids wake up and are fretful. We try playing guessing games. We try singing. My insides are mush. My mind rehearses John's disappearance. Everything is my fault. What were we doing here? How could I have been so stupid? My heart pounds and I find both breathing and swallowing difficult.

A taste of bitterness forms at the back of my throat. Where is the God of Israel now? Well, where was he when Job called? He surely was not going to explain. Not to Job and not to me. Explanation had never been this God's forte. "Get on with it!" is the best you ever get!

Two hours later, John reappears with an anxious Ada, six-year-old Arnon and Carmel. Ada is visibly upset because they have lost Rolfie, her huge black Belgian shepherd.

"The shelling terrified him and he ran off," John whispers to me, and I cannot help but feel great relief that we need not house the large beast in our now very narrow and already overpopulated quarters.

"The shelling started as soon as we left Arnona," John tells me. "We had to stop on the way in Shimon's grocery store." In continued murmur, he relates how an elderly couple had joined them, and how they all hovered behind the counter. Shimon had let the couple in and had asked them what they were doing out there. Didn't they know that there was a war going on?

"A war?" says the elderly gentleman. "You call this a war? You should have been in Budapest in 1942."

We share the story with Chavie, and there is a moment of lightheartedness and soft laughter as all of us contemplate the mild insanity of our collective history and of human inadequacies.

On Tuesday, June 6, *Galey Zahal* lets us know that fighting is going on at all fronts. The voice of Chaim Herzog[4] speaks soothingly to us in Irish-lilting English. "It is well to remember," he admonishes. "It is well to remember that the Egyptian army has not always been tremendously well organized."

Yes, it was definitely *well to remember*. For years afterwards, whenever nerves or disaster struck, Chaim Herzog's voice would enter and re-enter my mind. *It is well to remember that you are lucky to be alive. It is well to remember that you can still love. It is well to remember that life is short. Yes, it is well to remember...*

Chavie, Tahl and Offer leave us to join Dodah Marta, whose shelter is much larger and better supplied than ours. Chavie goes, but she leaves us the gun in its green bag. Soon she amazingly returns to tell us that we have all been invited to the larger and better-equipped shelter of the Cahanne family.

We try to walk fast down the familiar street, which has strangely changed its form, and appears to be some sort of torn asunder dystrophic futurama strewn with fallen electric wires, unfamiliar rubble and much debris. Nothing looks real. We hear airplanes overhead. Are they ours? Theirs? John worries about the kids stepping on the electric wiring. There is the constant sound of shelling from somewhere.

The Cahanne shelter seems huge and well furnished. There are chairs and sleeping bags for all of us. We are now eighteen: Dodah Marta and her husband, who is a veterinarian and is known to me only as Dr. Cahanne; Chavie and her two boys. There are Ada and her two children; John and I with our three girls, and we have also been joined by our neighborhood physician, Dr. Israel Lichtenstejn, his wife Hanna, and their two boys: seven-year-old

Ariel, and five-year-old Michael. Dr. Lichtenstejn takes charge assigning us chairs and sleeping spots. Cribs are found for Tammy and Carmel. Dodah Marta spreads a tablecloth on the floor. We are all to wash our hands and have seats around the pretend table. Somehow crackers and fruit appear. All of us have happily assumed the roles of nursery school children in Dodah Marta's care and under the supervision of Doctor Lichtenstejn. Nobody seems to mind in the slightest. We are all reduced to the trepidation of lost and bewildered childhood. Chaim Herzog on the radio continues to tell, "that it is well to remember Zahal's many talented fighter pilots."

At night I am woken up by a baby's cry. It takes me a minute to get oriented. I wonder why Ada isn't waking up to pick up Carmel, when I realize that it is not Carmel who is crying but my own Tammy. Tammy had been weaned, but I take her to my breast again. She sucks hungrily and returns to sleep. Her little body so intimately bound to mine is a consoling benediction.

Sometime during the night, I think that I am the only one awake. Dodah Marta approaches me. "I feel so horrible," she tells me in a whisper. "I simply had to turn them away."

"Who?" I whisper back.

"The Lurie family. They have nine children, you know. I don't know how long this is going to last. I just couldn't let them in. I told them to go to the nuns. They have a big shelter over there, and there isn't anyone else over there now, you know. Just three nuns. Still..." She holds her breath.

We look at one another in total understanding. I have nothing to say to her, but she knows that I, of all people, would understand her dilemma. At this point in our mutual history, I am no longer the dumb American. We are two Holocaust survivors, one from Czechoslovakia, the other from Poland. We see each other clearly across a chasm of horror. We see dread framed in heavy irony.

The Lurie family, Jews from one of the Arab countries, are a multi-generational family. They run a large and successful grocery at the corner of Korey Hadorot and Ein Ghedi streets. Both Dodah Marta and I have hosted, fed, and occasionally washed up a Lurie child. Ruthie Lurie is my personal favorite. She is bright, lively, and very creative. She is terrific when it comes to organizing birthday parties.

The German Convent is right across the street from the Lurie grocery. The nuns are German women who run a place evidently meant to serve Holocaust survivors in Jerusalem. They are part of the German *Wiedergutmachung* restitution program. The thought of turning Jews away in their hour of need to be housed in a shelter run by German nuns is a subject so loaded with contradictions, emotions, ambivalences and sorrow that truly it can truly only be spoken about in whispers between two women in the darkness of night. It cannot be brought out into the light of day.

On Wednesday, June 7, we listen breathlessly when the radio asks us to please remain in shelters. In unbelieving states of incredulity, we hear that the old city of Jerusalem, including the streets that for centuries had been "the Jewish Quarter" as well as the Western Wall of Solomon's and Herod's temples are all now in Israeli hands. We look at each other in wonder, and try to decipher the bewilderment that we read in one another's eyes.

"It is well to remember," Chaim Herzog's gentle radio voice warns, "that a war isn't over until it is over."

Meanwhile, it is well to remember that we are still alive. Yes, we are alive. We and our children have once more been given the great fortune, the great opportunity, the amazing possibility to continue our lives. "Blessed be thou Lord our God, king of the universe, source of all life, who has guarded us, kept us, and sustained us to this moment."

To life!

During the day, Dr. Cahanne disappears. We wonder. Dodah Marta does not seem particularly worried. "I guess she knows her husband," we tell one another.

At night, he returns. "Do you know where I have been?" he

asks. Mischief and schoolboy naughtiness percolate through his voice. Nobody dares to guess. Dr. Cahanne takes a deep breath before making his proclamation "I wanted to do it once before I died," he says. "I just had to do it. Today, ladies and gentlemen, I visited the Rockefeller Museum in old Jerusalem."

A stunned silence follows his announcement and then there is simultaneous applause. We laugh. We hug him. We hug one another. The Rockefeller Museum like the rest of the old city has for over 20 years been forbidden territory. The alleys of the market, the American Colony hotel, the Mosques of Omar and Al Aksa, and of course the wall—that wailing wall; that western wall of the temple; that one and only remainder of what had once been our glory, that great symbol of our magnificence, our downfall and our disasters, the place of Jewish longing and centuries of Jewish prayer and pilgrimage.

All that has so long, so very long been like a far-away moon landscape for us. Like some long forgotten dream. Like a mind-boggling narrative that was yet wasn't—the unreachable and unknown. Sometimes we would climb on the highest rooftops of our city to get a glimpse of the "over there" over there in Jordan—a place where we were not allowed to set foot. A place that certainly in our own lifetime we would never visit, never see; perhaps our children... our grandchildren, and yet here was Dr. Cahanne. He had been asked to stay in his shelter, but he had just taken the day off, off to be a tourist—dear God, he had visited the Rockefeller Museum on that other side—the side that now again was ours.

In all the days that followed the Six-Day war, in all the times when I did my shopping in the old city, in all the times when I visited The Western Wall and to this very day when I visit it, I have never gotten over how "close" these places are, how easily approachable.

"Close to what?" the younger generation asks. "Far away from what?"

135

It is impossible to tell them about the long journeys of time and of spirit.

On Thursday, June 8, we are officially allowed to step out of the shelter. All eighteen of us gather in Dodah Marta's garden. The kids make good use of the slide and swing set. Dodah Marta offers apples. We eat with relish, but as soon as planes are heard overhead, the kids grab hands and dash for the shelter.

"Ours, ours," Dodah Marta intones, no need to run, but the kids pay no heed. Their fear has been internalized. The radio tells us that Israel is consolidating its hold of the West Bank.

Where is that, we wonder. *What's there? What's there in that unknown land so close by?*

In the afternoon, tanks start rolling home downward from Kibbutz Ramat Rachel on the border on to Kore Hadorot Street. Dodah Marta hands out Israeli flags to the kids, who stand on the sidewalks waving the flags. Everywhere people are crawling out of their various holes of safety.

Someone starts the kids singing, *David Melech Israel* (David King of Israel) and *Chava Nagila* (Come, let us rejoice). Someone starts tossing flowers onto the returning tanks. On top of one of the tanks I spot the young soldier whom, a few days earlier—an eternity now it seems—I had seen fumbling with the cannon on the Lazarus lot. He is perched on top of one of the tanks arms raised in victorious salute. Nothing can describe the glow of his smile. His entire body radiates the joy of victory; the relief of regained life. Flowers rest in his curly hair. The world surely does love winners, but never quite as much as when pulled from the doom of disaster behind a poorly functioning cannon.

On Friday, June 9, there is heavy fighting on the Golan, but we can now return home. The streets are already being cleaned up. My kitchen is in a state of disarray. The large copper tray above the sink is full of holes, and has to come down. The freezer part of the fridge has the mark of shrapnel on it, but amazingly, both fridge and freezer are working. On the counter stands the grocery carton with my Monday's grocery purchases and my wallet. Is four days enough for the universe to shift? Of course it is. It happens all the time.

In the carton on the kitchen counter the vegetables have been completely smashed, but the milk is still there in its plastic bag. It has, of course, turned sour. Who can blame it? Then there is my lovely American wallet bought at Filene's basement in Boston. One half is in smithereens, the other side completely intact. The American side with my social security card, my American driver's license, and my voter registration card are all pulverized.

On the other side, my Israeli I.D., and the American Culture Center library card are unharmed. Heavy symbolism there, I suppose, but I don't have the luxury of contemplating it. The house needs a thorough cleaning. It's wonderful to be back in my own home. Amazingly, the washing machine, which usually breaks down, starts up with the turn of the dial.

The girls are re-discovering their own room next to the kitchen. Their old toys are all of a sudden alluring. Tammy stands in her crib. As long as she has big sisters to watch she will be happy.

I open the kitchen door and step out into the back yard. Tammy's diapers are still out there but they are full of holes made by the flying shrapnel. I take them down mumbling a prayer as each pair of clothespins drops into my apron pocket. I sweep the kitchen floor trying to figure out what and how to make supper. First I must change Tammy's diaper.

Saturday, June 10, Israel gains control of the Golan Heights, and I visit with my friend, Eva Oesterman. The Oestermans did not have a shelter. They chose to stay behind shuttered windows. Everyone is out in the street comparing notes. Everyone has a story to tell, but only one thing is obvious: We don't live on the border anymore. The real-estate value of our homes is up, and what's more we are all drunk with relief.

John has gone to work at the Hebrew University. He returns in a daze later in the afternoon. There are hints that his temporary job has suddenly become a permanent one. Someone evidently noticed and appreciated the fact that we stayed. That night we can sleep in our own bed again. We make madly passionate, satisfying love, and sleep like drunken bears.

A week later, I walk to Steinmetsky's English Bookstore on Ben Yehuda Street in central Jerusalem, where I buy the most recent issue of *Time Magazine*. Among the letters to the editor is one in which the correspondent asks for the address of General de Gaulle so that he, letter writer, can send the worthy general quotes from the previous issue. The letter writer wants to send the general's predictive words between two pieces of Matza, so that the general might eat his words in greater comfort.

People have often asked me whether I had ever had serious guilt and regrets about having stayed in Israel at the time, about deliberately putting my children in "harm's way." But "harm's way" is an interesting concept. We spent 24 years in Israel, 22 of these were in post-Six-Day-war. We lived in Jerusalem during the much more danger-filled Yom Kippur war.

But during all those years neither we, nor our children ever truly felt a sense of peril, even though all of us frequently wandered about empty and dark streets of Jerusalem when returning late from seminars, scout activities, or other work or school-connected events. Nothing dreadful ever happened to any of us in war-torn Israel.

However, in our later American life, John and I were mugged and John was badly beaten up one morning as we were peacefully jogging in a "good" neighborhood of Tucson Arizona, and a careless driver in nonviolent and well-behaved Yuma, Arizona killed John.

Life moves about in its peculiar way and we move with it, making our plans, living our ideals, and so often truly believing that we are in control of things. "Man plans and God laughs," says the old Yiddish proverb.

THE BALABUSTA

Ever heard the word *balabusta*? In Yiddish[1] it means a superb housewife.

"Every woman should first strive to be a balabusta," my Aunt Dora once told me. "You can be a brain surgeon or a nuclear physicist, but first of all, you must be a balabusta."

And my poor Aunt Dora strived mightily to fill that bill. The balabusta is the woman of valor, so praised in Jewish Sabbath liturgy.

"A woman of valor, who can find her? Her worth is far above Jewels.
The heart of her husband trusts in her, and nothing shall he lack."
(Proverbs 31).

Who can live with that on the menu? Not I, let me tell you. However, when I lived in Israel, my Russian downstairs neighbor, Julia, had a better definition: "A balabusta is a woman in whose home one never runs out of toilet paper."

Now that was a definition I could accept, and it has stayed with me for about 30 years. This, unfortunately, was the case before my

Swedish niece Elizabeth, whom I dearly love, together with her girlfriend Johanna, visited me in Philadelphia.

First of all, you should know that Elizabeth's mother, Agneta, is Finish, but has lived in Sweden for most of her adult life. Swedish women are on the whole natural balabustas and a Finish Swede, unsurprisingly, in her immigrant status, is placed in a position where she must outdo the Swedes. Agneta is married to my foster-brother, Sven, and she is the absolute and ultimate balabusta. Agneta's house simply sparkles. The food she prepares isn't just tasty. It's delicious to the utmost degree.

But there is more. Agneta's dishes are also served beautifully, and it all seems to emerge on the table with magic. When do the potatoes get peeled? When does the soup get stirred? When do the sausages sizzle to perfection? How does the sauce receive its smoothness? Agneta performs her balabusta magic, and she, of course, does it with the balabusta smile. *"She tends to the affairs of her household, and eats not the bread of idleness... her deeds speak her praise."* (Proverbs, 31:10-31), and Elizabeth is, of course, Agneta's daughter, and, as I must duly note, she too is definitely a balabusta—if still, only such, in training.

So, you can well imagine how hard I tried to be the best balabusta hostess I could possibly be during Elizabeth's visit. The fridge was stocked. The sheets were folded (though not ironed) at the bedstead. The bathroom had been thoroughly scrubbed and the oven had unbelievably self-cleaned. Not even my computer was dusty.

The two young women were lovely guests. They went sightseeing in Philadelphia. They saw the historical things, and particularly enjoyed the Constitution Center. They chatted amicably with oldsters. They shopped and were amazed at the good prices at Gap and at Macy's. They visited Starbucks (imagine, there was still no Starbucks in Sweden) and on the whole, they seemed pleased. Thus, you can well imagine my utter humiliation when on their last night in my house the absolutely unspeakable occurred.

One afternoon, Elizabeth accosted me with that well-known, but quite insignificant cardboard scroll in her very Swedish balabusta hand and a slightly questioning expression on her beautiful Finish-Swedish face. "Where," she wondered, "do you keep your toilet paper?"

Well, as I have told you, this was one aspect of balabustaship on which I considered myself quite worthy, and without the slightest hesitation and somewhat indulgent pretension, I directed my Northern guest to my small, but well-equipped laundry room, where among other thing such as garbage bags and paper towels I had always kept sufficient and ample supply of the required resource. Being the good guest she was, Elizabeth spent quite a bit of time inspecting the contents of the place, which she pronounced to be excellent use of urban dwelling, but unfortunately, she couldn't find what she was looking for. Had I actually run out of toilet paper?

Frantically I looked and looked. Yes, it was true. I had been sure of two enormous packages—each containing several rolls— what could have happened to them? How was this possible? I was actually out of toilet paper. In a state of frenzy, I tossed a box of Kleenex to Elizabeth, as I dashed downstairs to my downstairs grocery and was back in a flash and with an outburst of apologies. This, my friends, should not have happened!

Thus, my balabusta life ended, even as two weeks later, in search of ammonia, I discovered the two missing packets behind the dryer. Inanimate objects do plot against you. Take my word for it! And I am still vying for the balabusta label.

ALI AND HIS ISRAELI TEACHER

We left Israel in 1988. Ostensibly, it was just for a sabbatical. We had saved up for a two-year leave-of-absence, and John found a job in Arizona. Life is, of course, full of all kinds of twists and turns. We wound up staying in Arizona, where I did my Ph.D. in literature at the University of Arizona and taught ESL at the CESL (Center for English as a Second Language) at the University of Arizona.

When Ali arrived in my 60-level class at CESL in the fall of 1990, I got a bit of a stomachache. Of course, by this time, I had gotten used to Arab students, in my classes, but Ali was different. Sandy-haired and blue-eyed, he reminded me of many of the Israeli kids I had taught at the Hebrew Gymnasia in Jerusalem. He was a Palestinian from Jerusalem. For all I knew, he could have been a neighbor.

It was my second year at the University of Arizona, and I was beginning to feel and act like a native. At any rate, Ali certainly never suspected that his nice American teacher, who so much reminded him of his mother, could possibly also be an evil Israeli. Mind you, there were times when I thought he knew. For example, on his second day in class he told me that a local radio station had asked to interview him about the intifada.[1]

"You think good for me to talk about it for the all world?" he wondered.

"Well, how do you feel about it?" I asked.

"I think it very important," he said. "*People* here. They so ignorant. Have no idea what happen over there and how cruel the Israelis are."

He knows, I said to myself, as various internal organs began to crunch.

"Well, if you feel that it's so important, then I guess you should do it," I told him with what I hoped was a straight and possibly indifferent teacher face.

"You not understand," he said. "You Americans are so..." He searched for the word.

"Naive," I supplied.

"Just it!" he agreed enthusiastically (I should know. For my 24 years in Israel I was known as 'Natalie-ha-naeevit'—Natalie the naive, the dumb American).

"Israeli spies everywhere," Ali told me. "If I talk on radio, someone make tape, and I never can to return my own country. Maybe even my mother. She will have *broblems*."

Perhaps he was right. I was, after all, just a naive teacher of English. What did I know?

"It's always good to be careful," I told him.

We got along splendidly–Ali and I. He made rapid progress in English. He was the life of the class. The Japanese girls thought him "hot," or was it "cool" in that day's vernacular? I do remember that a Mexican girl, Marcella, was ready to introduce him to her parents and to send money to needy Palestinian children.

And, best of all, Ali appreciated my communicative strategies. He kept writing his mother about how lucky he was to have such a fine teacher. He showed me the letters, written in Arabic, and he translated. There were whole transcripts of class activities. He knew that his mother, who was a supervisor of teachers, would appreciate these.

Once, unable to resist, I asked him if he spoke Hebrew. He did. Like I had once done, Ali got his Hebrew at an *ulpan* (Intensive Hebrew language course. These are found throughout Israel for the benefit of newcomers). He was full of contempt for the institution. "No good teaching." The teacher, a young man of some vague European descent, hadn't liked Ali. He had been in a class full of Russian-Jewish immigrants who toted guns in a display of their newly found patriotism and, quickly having forgotten what it was like to be members of a minority, had treated him badly.

Thank goodness, I thought, *at least Ali's mother isn't a teacher of English.*

I had been very active in the English teachers' organization, and I had trained both Arab and Jewish teachers all over Jerusalem. Keeping a secret identity was not exactly easy for me. It brought back too many painful memories. Nevertheless, that is what I had decided to do after my first summer at CESL.

That summer I had a level 70 class that represented the usual CESL mix—a third Arabs, a third Mexicans, and a third Japanese in addition to two Europeans. In the usual way, we all introduced ourselves on the first day and said where we were from. I had happily announced that I was from Israel. There was some visual tension, but no immediate repercussions and the class work proceeded in what appeared to be fairly pleasant and normal pace.

But, in mid-term one morning as I was walking up the stairs absorbed in my own thoughts the word, "*Yahood*," (Jew in Arabic) hit me like biting hail. Several Arab students stood about on the staircase and in the entry hall. I wasn't sure where the sound had started. I knew that it was being variously repeated, and a deep fear that I had long since forgotten, but that I recognized, gnarled at my innards. My feet moved heavily up the staircase. I made it to class where the usual dynamics of the classroom took over. Ahmed, Mohamed, Anwar and Salah were just students. Not different from

Hernando or Yoko; not different from Yoram and Dalit either for that matter.

It was only at the end of the course that I was approached by an Arab delegation. They had bought me a present, and considering the state of the world, they were being very kind. They told me how much they had enjoyed my class. They also told me that they had almost walked out of class on that very first day when I had told them that I was Israeli. That was the last time I told.

In Ali's case, things didn't get bad until he started turning in journals. Naturally they were full of anti-Israel sentiments and anti-Jewish feeling. I had, of course, expected this but not quite in such mythical proportions. The Jews of Ali's journals were the children of Satan—intrinsically and fundamentally evil. There was only one solution to the Jewish problem—the one Hitler unfortunately had not had time enough to carry out. Such sentiments were juxtaposed on the certainty that the Holocaust had never existed. It was a Jewish fabrication to enlist international sympathy. America was controlled by the Jewish press and Jewish bankers. The Israelis had started wars against all their neighbors. The only border on which they had not fought was the Mediterranean, and only fish lived in that sea, not really a suitable enemy for the fearsome Israelis.

Ali's dreams and nightmares were full of Jewish soldiers chasing him along the narrow alleyways and market lanes of Jerusalem's old city. His bogeymen all wore the Star of David.

It took me a while to develop a system through which I could react to Ali's writings. Eventually, I adopted a philosophy of broad-minded neutrality. I told him that history was never an objective matter, and that basically each historian cheered for his own team. I suggested that there might be two sides to every story. I offered a future utopian vision in which race and nation would no longer serve as categorizing devices and I suggested conflict resolution schemes.

Ali responded to my musings with tolerant condescension—I

was, after all, a naive American. And I did remind him of his mother, to whom, it turned out, he had not been very nice in the months and weeks before he left for America. His kindness to me, I assumed, was his curious way of making reparation.

A few weeks into the term someone told Ali that one of his teachers was Jewish. For some reason Ali assumed that it was Elaine Burns, his very blond and very WASP writing teacher. One day as I was innocently passing from my office to the faculty lounge, I was pushed toward a group of students and teachers, whose loud and tension-filled voices trumpeted turbulence. My tendency to timidity as a rule quickly moves me away from any such commotion. This time I was inexorably propelled toward it.

In the middle of a circle of agitated students and faculty, Ali was loudly accusing Elaine of having unfairly graded him because she was Jewish and he was Arab. Elaine had become thoroughly indignant and would have none of it. She was not Jewish. She was married to a Lebanese, and furthermore, had she been Jewish, how did Ali dare to assume that she would be so prejudiced! She demanded an apology, and much to my amazement, she got one from a rather flustered and embarrassed Ali. I, for one, couldn't wait to disappear to the sanctuary of the teachers' lounge where the only noise was a soft hum from the newly purchased photocopying machine.

At mid-term I had to go to England for ten days. I was scheduled to work on a British Council teacher-training seminar in Canterbury with my friend and mentor Tessa Woodward. I had looked forward to this experience for some time, and now that it would give me respite from the tensions engendered by Ali's presence, I was even happier about the jaunt. Ali was scheduled to give a speech during the time I was gone, and since I knew the anti-Israeli content of his presentation, I begged my substitute, Diana, to make sure that the thing would be over by the time I got back.

When I returned to Tucson, Diana was thoroughly apologetic. "I really tried to make him do it," she said. "I didn't just try. I worked on it! But there was no way. You must believe me, Natalie. He insisted that Mrs. Hess had to hear his speech. He traded time slots first with Rodrigo and then with Mieko. He was adamant Mrs. Hess had to hear his speech. There was absolutely nothing I could do about it!"

The speech was a worse trial for me than I had anticipated. It was entitled "Cry my beloved country" and it included all the material from his journals and then some. Ali was a good speaker, and the drawing he made on the board of the little land we both so loved was much better than anything I could have drawn. His view of the world spoke to the hearts of the students. They were full of wonder and questions.

When I asked each of them to speak about something that had particularly impressed them, many of them wished Ali luck in his struggle against the giants of evil that now ever-so-temporarily were in possession of his beloved home. There was only one small and slightly dissenting voice. Mieko from Japan said that the speech had indeed been very impressive, but that she would be interested in hearing the Israeli point of view. To which Ali with gentlemanly flair answered, "You entitled!"

I could have hugged little Mieko. If she only knew how close and how yearning to burst out that Israeli point of view was! I gave Ali an "A" on his speech and wrote that his vocabulary had greatly increased. I also corrected a few grammar and pronunciation mistakes.

When the bell rang, Ali moved toward my desk. He was obviously in search for more praise. Luckily, he was soon surrounded by students who had questions to ask him, and I was able to make a quick get-away to my office.

The place was empty and I was finally able to cry. For a whole hour the sobs kept coming—huge and relentless. Then it was over. Later, when my husband asked me why I had cried, I had a difficult time explaining it. Had I just been crying to relieve tension? Had I been crying about the utter impossibility of Jewish history? Or had I simply been delving into existential frustrations?

As our session drew to its end, Iraq invaded Kuwait. Many of the Arab students at CESL expressed concern over the events. We were on our way to view an exhibit of Indian pottery, when Ali told me how happy he was about the invasion. He took some time explaining to me how the Sabahs, Kuwait's ruling family, had abused their power and how good it was that someone finally was strong enough to get rid of them, and the next step, Ali assured me, would be Israel. Sadam Hussein was the savior who would free Palestine. How could Ali possibly know that my worst nightmares speculated on the same results?

Ali made plans to remain at the University of Arizona, and I knew, of course, had known for some time that I would have to tell him. I decided to do it the minute he was not longer my student. There was a class party, gifts, and a card signed by all the students. Ali had signed his name on top of the list and I suspected that he was the one who had organized the party. I got hugs and kisses; there was dancing and there were games. The students brought national foods and some dressed in national costumes. We took pictures and Ali wanted some with me.

"To send my mother!"

The following day I was cleaning out my desk, when Ali sauntered in wanting to chat, and I knew that the moment had come.

"Sit down, Ali," I said, "I have something rather important to talk to you about." The seriousness of my voice made his blue eyes grow wider. He sat down.

"This is going to be a little difficult for you, Ali," I said, "And it is also very difficult for me, but the time has come and I have to tell you."

From the display of unease of his face, I could tell that Ali was growing intensely fearful, and suddenly I felt very sorry for him. In an unanticipated rush of emotion, I saw him as the 19-year-old child away from home that he was and impulsively I put my arm around him.

"It's nothing terrible," I said. "Nothing bad is going to happen." And surprisingly the whole thing seemed trivial and ridiculous to me. "I just wanted to tell you that I am Jewish."

There was silence. Thick and heavy.

Ali's jaw literally dropped. His eyes grew round and enormous. He didn't utter a sound. He looked like a frightened baby and again I felt tremendously sorry for him, yet at the same time I felt an absolutely overwhelming need to pour it all out and be done with it!

"And there is more," I said. "I am a Holocaust survivor. Yes, the Holocaust really happened. I know because I was there. Also, I am an Israeli. I lived in Israel for 24 years, 22 in Jerusalem. I still have a house there and my three daughters live there."

Ali only stared. Then he groaned. Finally he stood up and turned around. He fled from the room, and I felt thoroughly guilty and then I was afraid.

The next day, Ali's name had been scratched out from the greeting card that stood on my desk. There was also a long letter from Ali. He had gone to talk to a number of teachers and a number of students.

It turned out that everyone knew, everyone except him (that one really surprised me). Why hadn't anyone told him? Why hadn't I told him? That just went to show how treacherous everyone was. Ali wrote "everyone," but, of course, he meant the Jews, and he actually used the word "treacherous." His vocabulary really had grown by leaps and bounds!

The next time I saw him was on the campus mall. He looked pathetically small and scared, and when I reached out a hand to him, he took it.

"Ali," I said, "what would you have done if you had been in my shoes?"

"Did you photocopy my journals and send them to Israel?" he asked.

The idea was so ridiculous that I burst out laughing. "Are you planning to send me a letter bomb?" I asked.

This time it was Ali who laughed.

We wound up having frozen yogurt together. He was, of course more frightened than I, and poor baby, he had reason to be. Nevertheless, it was a revelation to him that I too was scared and that my husband had advised me not to tell him. After all, my job was to teach him English, and that I had done rather well. Political persuasions were just not part of the game and should be left out.

"Then why did you decide to tell me?" Ali wondered.

"I heard that you were making plans to stay at the University of Arizona and I knew that sooner or later you would find out and then you would think that I tricked you terribly, so I thought it would be better for me to tell you."

"I thought you like me," he said wistfully.

"I did," I said. "I do! That's one reason I had to tell you."

"But all the terrible things I said. You must feel so bad."

"I did," I said. "You made me cry."

"So then how can you like me?" he said.

"The same way you like me," I said. "If I were a Palestinian boy of nineteen years, I would probably feel exactly the same way you do."

"Cheering for your own team," he said, quoting me, and I felt the tremendous pride a teacher feels when a student actually demonstrates remembering something she has taught.

The next day Ali came by my office to invite me to lunch. "If you are not afraid of being poisoned by a Palestinian," he said, "I know of a great place to buy falafel, you know it?"

I didn't. It was a cozy upstairs patio place run by—guess who?—a Palestinian. Interestingly, Ali had not told the owner, whose name was Hammed, of his own origin. Was Ali too beginning to find need for a secret identity? Partially at least, it turned out to be so.

As I grew to know Ali better (he stayed on at CESL for another eight weeks), I discovered that he had problems with "my Arab brethren" as he was to call them. A Palestinian Arab was, it seemed, quite a stranger in the Arab world. Ali's outlook on the lives of women, on politics, and even on Islam, was different from mainline Arab attitudes. Like it or not, Jews and Arabs in Israel had influenced each other's ways of seeing the world, and that in turn influenced the way Ali and I related to each other.

Soon Ali and I were talking to each other in Hebrew. His Hebrew was not nearly as good as his English, but having a secret code gave us a key to secret understandings. We both began enjoying it. I was the only person at CESL who could understand the pleasure Ali took in spending a weekend browsing in a large American supermarket, or who could understand his sense of disorientation on the American freeway, or his delight at the quantity and quality of jeans at the discount outlet. He had spent a year in Jerusalem working as a tax accountant. There was terminology that he knew in Hebrew, but didn't know in English— words like mortgage, foreclosure, interest, and capital. I felt good about being able to supply these, and then there were times when Ali thought of a word in Hebrew before I did. He got a tremendous charge out of that!

We were meeting to chat on a fairly regular basis by then, and Ali's attacks on Israel and the Israelis had assumed what I would call a down to earth rather than a doctrinaire tone.

"The stupid idiots don't even know how to make out their own income tax forms," he told me. "It's a joke, the money they pay me to do it for them."

"Me too!" I told Ali. "I'm the worst of the lot. I'll pay you to do mine."

"I'll do yours for free," he generously offered.

He told me that before he had known, he had envisioned

having me visit Jerusalem and being my tourist guide there. "What a joke!"

I suggested that we still might do it. He would show me his favorite parts of the Arab quarter and I would do the same with the Jewish quarter. We both knew that the notion was somewhat farfetched in the political climate of the day, as Jews didn't dare to set foot in Arab quarters and Arabs had their documents inspected when they wandered into Jewish sections of town.

But from a table at Carol's Frozen Yogurt in Tucson, Arizona it sounded feasible and fun. Ali complained to me that he had always been spotted as an Arab when he entered the Jewish part of town. He asked me how the Jews always knew, and I didn't know the answer. But when my daughter from Jerusalem visited, she told me right away. "It's his haircut and his shoes," she said, and we both wondered whether or not we should tell Ali. Was the situation one of personal friendship or one of national security risk?

There was a day when he asked me about the Holocaust and when I brought him *The Diary of Anne Frank*. He cried when he read it—just like everyone else does.

I found myself singularly unmoved by his tears. Later, I wondered about that. Well, everyone cries when reading a sad story. Does it mean that one believes in the story? I doubt it.

A few weeks later, Ali left Tucson to go and study at Arizona State University in Phoenix. For a while, we called each other. When the peace process started, for example, we both felt the need to talk. When I was in Jerusalem, I tried to look up his family, but although they knew all about me, they didn't want to meet me. I understood, and I hoped that one day it just might be different. The way it got to be different for Ali and me.

PART 5
BECOMING A WIDOW

WHO IS WILLA?

My world collapsed on Monday April 25th, 2011, but the weird thing is that I wake up that morning feeling unexpectedly happy.

My cousin Zora and her husband, Bill, who had visited us for the Passover week, had left on Saturday. Our daughter, Rebecka, and the grandchildren from Philadelphia, had left on Sunday. The visits had been successful, and now we are back to our own lives. Just John and Natalie in our together life on a beautiful morning.

Two pleasant ladies are guests in the over-large house that we, some years ago, had turned into a bed-and-breakfast. I serve them breakfast, and clean up the kitchen. I change from my homey-hostess clothes to my professional dress-with-pearls. I am feeling put-together and efficient, as John and I walk to the car.

For some reason, he opens the car door for me, which is not something he usually does, and before I manage to move into my seat, he kisses me, and I look up to see the love in his eyes.

I have replayed that moment many times in my mind since then, and from that memory I have learned that one is not really alive unless one sees oneself loved in another person's eyes. I didn't know it then. I was spoiled. I took so much for granted, yes, dear God, I took ever so much for granted.

Driving to work, we enjoy the inside-bubble-feeling of relaxed conversation that one has in the secluded and insular atmosphere of a car. John is an excellent driver, while I have always been a wimpy one. He taught me how to drive right after we married, but since he always enjoyed the role of "chauffeur," my driving skills remained limited.

April 25, 2011 is, as I said, an unusually lovely day in Yuma, Arizona. The sun is an embracing presence and not the devil's eye-in-the-sky that it will later become. Our yellow lantana is blooming and the bougainvillea on the side of the house is picking up. John has just mowed our small front lawn and watered the grapefruit and lemon trees.

I am grateful to be back in my office. Everything seems under control and nothing is particularly urgent. I go to a colleague's office to talk about a project we are working on.

At one, John comes to pick me up. We have lunch at Café 95, a Thai-Chinese, popular hole-in-the-wall where the food is delicious, the service efficient, and the enticing cooking aroma greets us in the parking lot. As usual, we order the war-wonton soup, which is a blend of everything but the proverbial kitchen sink bonded by a fabulous Asian broth, and we also split a chicken-mango dish served with steamed white rice and hot tea—a combination that is one of our favorites.

I look at John as he sits opposite me and think how handsome he is in his blue-checked shirt. I remember his long hands marked by liver spots reaching out for me from across the table. I remember nudging his sandaled feet with mine and telling him once again how much I love him and what a good deal we have, and how cute I think he is and smiling at his standard reply, "You are much cuter."

John is not really listening to me. He is in the distant mode I know so well, and I have reached his automatic pilot B-level attention, but his eyes have that faded-out look, which I recognize, and I know that although he finishes his food with relish down to the last morsel, he probably has not enjoyed it as much as I have enjoyed mine. His thoughts are elsewhere, most likely on the thermo-dynamics project that has lately grabbed his interest and which he hopes to somehow attach to a business plan involving solar energy.

"Darling," I say, "You are fading out on me."

"I know." He grins. "But I think that I might be getting close to something."

At that moment I am glad that a new interest has come his way, even though I also want him with me in the flavorful pleasure of the present moment.

And while I am still reveling in the lusciousness of the food, John drives me back to work.

As we move up to the college parking lot, I suddenly, and for no reason at all, think about the two ladies who are, at the moment, staying at our Bed and Breakfast. One of the ladies is called Tam. I remember her name because our youngest daughter is named Tamar, but, for the life of me, I cannot remember the second lady's name, and amazingly, John, who as a rule doesn't remember these socially related issues, unhesitatingly tosses the name to me.

"Her name is Willa."

"How on earth did you remember that?" I wonder. It is an unusual name, and John, as far as I know, has never been a Willa Cather fan.

"I once had a girlfriend in high school called Willa," he says, and I am hit by the thought that there is still much about John's life that even after 53 years of marriage I still don't know.

"Will you tell me about Willa tonight?" I ask.

His smile holds a riddle. "There isn't that much," he says. "But yes, tonight, I'll tell you about Willa."

I still I don't know about Willa. Can I Google her? Is she on Facebook? Does she tweet? Did she marry a Supreme Court justice and have seven sons? Did she change her name? Is she gay? Is she transgender? Is she a loving grandmother?

"Hey, there, world of Willas. Which one of you was the girlfriend of my husband, John Hess, when he was in high school in the 1950s? You remember John Hess, don't you? He was that tall, gangly, cute kid, who was so good in math. He was the first in the city on one of those huge math exams. You remember that one for sure, don't you? Please tell me about the John you knew. Did you like him? Did you think that you would marry him? Please speak out, Willa, you were one of the last things that my husband and I talked about."

There was still so very much to talk about.

I simply never considered the possibility of life without him. He would always be there to answer my questions. He could always be depended on.

Oh yes, of course, we did talk about death. We had often considered buying our burial plots in Israel, where two of our three daughters live, but it was so expensive. We could always use that money better for a present-day need, and there would surely be some money left over when we died, so we would just have to let the daughters take care of it.

"But if we buy the plots now, we could sit and have a picnic there," John had pointed out. "It would be our real-estate, after all."

That would get us into a fit of giggles.

"Hey, when we are there next to each other, can I reach out and play with your boobs?" John would ask.

"No!" I was always firm about that one.

Occasionally, when the issue emerged, I might grow philosophical, and remind him that the stuff that goes into a grave is just discarded old clothing.

"The real me and you will be somewhere else," I tell him.

"Where?" he would wonder.

I couldn't answer that one. I still can't. Judaism does not give us a clear geography for the afterlife. We have to invent our own. I still have not invented mine—not for my parents, not for my foster mother, and not for John, and yet I fully feel the presence of these people and cannot live in a life that denies it. Somewhere, somehow they are.

I had a rabbi once who insisted that all who had died were happily milling about, being sociable at a huge, heavenly Bar Mitzvah party or a Jewish wedding. "We do these things so well," the rabbi had insisted. "Surely, this will be our afterlife."

But John had hated these social occasions, so if this scene is what to be expected, he is not a happy camper, and I should be there to help him out the way I always did on social occasions.

When John drops me off at work, we usually stop in the parking lot for a while and chat. What do we usually talk about? It might be local politics, or about something that we are planning to send to our daughters, or about a book that we are both reading. Our political arguments can sometimes grow animated, not quite heated but nevertheless vigorous. John tends to pretty much take the liberal view. I feel that political friends of the moment must be accepted, even if not fully trusted.

But at this particularly crucial moment, on this particular day, on this Monday, just as I might find out more about Willa, my boss steps out the door of the Academic Complex, and I feel that remaining in the car is not good professional policy. I should be chatting up the boss, which is unfortunately exactly what I do.

Usually, when John turns the car around to pull out of the parking lot, I wave. I had done that in the morning. The ritual is a signal that all is well and that, no matter which words were exchanged, even if these were strident, we are in love; we will see each other again at the end of the day and we will make up in bed.

But, at this particular time, after lunch, because I start some semi-professional talk with the boss, I don't turn around. I don't take the time to stop, to turn around and wave.

For the rest of my life, I will be flooded with unrelenting remorse. If only I had stopped to chat in the car in my usual way. If only I had ignored the boss. If only both of us had stopped to wave, that sixteen-year-old would have passed through her stop sign before John reached his deadly encounter with her.

I return to the office and immerse myself in work, which involves a visit to the library. I check for phone messages and find no messages from John. He would usually leave a message sometime in the afternoon. I call home, and there in my ear is John's slow and carefully modulated voice on our recorded Bed and Breakfast message: "You have reached the Jenny Kent Bed and Breakfast. Please leave us a message. We will get back to you, just as soon as we can. Thank you."

I call his cell phone—no answer. My stomach begins to churn into its worry mode, and I am quick to pick up when the phone on my desk buzzes.

"Is this Mrs. Hess?" a nervous male voice asks. "Are you the wife of John Hess? Your husband has been involved in a traffic accident. Please come to the Yuma Medical Center hospital emergency ward."

And that is that. The nightmare that only happens to other people is suddenly mine. The world that was disappears.

FINALITY

I stand with the telephone receiver in my hand. I have to get to the hospital. Just a minute. Hold on. Think, girl. First, you have to get out to the parking lot and find the car. I dig in my pocket and feel the keys. I am out the door. But wait, the office door has to be locked. Students have to be notified. And then, just like that, I remember: I have no car. Why don't I have a car? John was supposed to pick me up.

Calling a taxi in Yuma, Arizona, usually means at least a half-hour wait. I have to ask someone to drive me to the hospital and I hate asking for favors; I hate asking for help. I never ask for help. I am the person who gives help, but now I have to ask for help. There is no other way. There just isn't. *Buckle up, girl. You have to go to ask for help! Just do it!*

I walk into the main office on jelly legs. I ask for help, and it is instantly offered. Bernardette Pressloid, a colleague, volunteers. "I have a class to teach this afternoon, Natalie, but I'm going to leave a message for my students. Don't worry about it. These are grad students. They'll wait for me."

So here I am, flooded with guilt. Work has always been

sacrosanct. That someone should be late for a class because of me is anathema, but it can't be helped.

"You don't know how grateful I am," I tell Bernadette as we rush through the parking lot.

"Oh, for heaven's sake, Natalie, It's absolutely nothing."

The afternoon traffic is not heavy, but our silent drive to the hospital seems endless. I feel that I should be making conversation, but I can't and I give up on trying and abandon myself to gnawing anxiety.

Bernadette offers to go with me into the emergency ward. I turn her down. After all, she has a class to teach. Inside, a bored clerk cannot find the name John Hess on his list.

"Are you sure we called you?" he asks.

"I hope you didn't," is my automatic reaction and relief floods through me. Perhaps it is a minor matter, after all, and he has already been discharged.

"Does he have a middle name?"

"Yes, Harris."

And that is how he has been listed, and that is how I find him— totally sedated and bound to a stretcher. They are planning to send him to a hospital in Phoenix.

"There seems to be a minor brain concussion," they tell me. The clerk puts stress on the word "minor" and I instantly grab at its comfort. They give me half an hour to get home in a cab "to get what you need."

Get what I need. What do I need? Tam and Willa, our bed-and-breakfast guests, are not to be seen. I write them a hasty note. They can stay as long as they want to. They will have to serve themselves breakfast, and lock up as they leave. They can leave the key with Mary, our neighbor. The morning's breakfast dishes are still in the sink.

I call my daughter Rebecka to give her the bad news. As usual she is to-the-point practical. As a single mom of two lively boys she has to be. "Which hospital are they taking you to, mom?"

162

"I don't know."

"Well, call me as soon as you do. And mom, don't forget your cell phone and the charger."

Good thing. I just might have forgotten. John was the one who carried the cell phone. John was the one who packed the charger. The stupid thing is that I always felt that I was picking up after him. It seems that he was the one who picked up after me. Still, why hadn't he put those breakfast dishes in the sink? And what kind of an idiot am I thinking about such things now?

I spend the next two weeks walking up and down sterile hospital corridors of St. Joseph's Hospital in Phoenix. At one point, I take off my shoes, and the nurse in charge reprimands me. "This is not a hotel, lady!"

John remains sedated. He is breathing with difficulty and they insert a breathing tube. His hands are tied down, I assume to keep him from moving the intricate tubing that surrounds him. During the first few days I am given great hope. They tell me that the brain injury indeed seems minor, and the machines all around him keep ticking. I don't have a clue about what is to happen.

My daughter Deborah calls from Haifa in Israel. "I'll be there on the next plane, mom."

"No darling, it's such an expensive trip. You really don't need to come. Dad and I will be home in a few days."

"I really do want to come, mom. I'll be there just as soon as I can."

I work hard to dissuade her but she insists.

I call Rebecka to tell her that Deb is coming, and doesn't she think that is a bit far-fetched and unnecessary. "No, mom," she tells me. "I am so glad that I have a sister who is willing and able to make it."

Tammy, my youngest, calls from Jerusalem. She apologizes for not being able to come. She has an important meeting. I tell her not to worry. "Daddy and I are doing fine," I tell her. "We should be home in a few days."

Strange as it seems, I really do believe this. John was always the healthy one. Surely this is something that will work itself out. Clearly, I am in a state of denial, but I don't know this. I just know that right now things are difficult, but surely it will all work out. Surely John will always be there for me.

Becky, who teaches veterinary medicine at the University of Pennsylvania and knows more about hospital life than the rest of us, cannot come, but she sends daily pizza for the nursing staff figuring that this just might improve the atmosphere around her father's bed. It actually seems to do that. The nurses become friendlier, a bit more human; or am I just imagining this?

During John's third night at the hospital, the breathing tube is removed and he gains consciousness. His first whispered request is for his hands to be untied.

"Untie... untie," he whispers and I obtain permission to do that. Later, he is delighted with the yellow shirt of his lovely young nurse, whose name, Shey, he repeats longingly over and over again. "Shey, Shey, Shey."

I am wildly jealous. Is this what he has always wanted? An amply-bosomed young woman in a yellow blouse?

At first, he doesn't recognize me and I am swamped by torrents of resentment. Why can't I be young and pretty in a yellow blouse for him now?

Later, he does recognize me and tells me, "I love you."

I repeat and he tells me that he loves me too. He remembers the names of our daughters and of his grandchildren. He remembers the dates of the Civil War. We had both just been reading a novel about the Civil War and he remembers the name of the heroine, Alex.

When asked what his address is, he gives the Jerusalem address we had more than 20 years earlier and he says it in Hebrew, *"Shlosh-Esre Giladi."*

He enunciates the words with ringing pride. He doesn't remember the name of our current president. I tell him over and over again that I love him. How very foolishly inadequate these declarations seem now. What an idiot I was to be jealous of the nurse. I even scold him in Hebrew for having set his eyes on young women, just like his flirtatious dad used to.

"Don't be like your dad," I tell him in Hebrew.

I am sure that we are headed for recovery and rehabilitation the following day. The hospital social worker has already talked to me about it.

John keeps repeating that he has to pee. "I have to pee," he insists with greater and greater urgency.

I show him the plastic tube that moves urine out and try to explain over and over again that he does not have to worry about peeing, but he only keeps repeating, "I have to pee. I have to pee."

I corner one of the young doctors to ask if I will have to get used to such repeated questions.

"Yes, that will be one of the stages of recovery, but be patient. Gradually such repetition is phased out."

I make plans to rent an apartment close to the hospital. I had not slept for two nights, as I wandered the halls of the hospital and sat by John's bed. The nurses had scolded me for doing too much floor pacing. Rebecka has kept constant contact by phone. She insists that I go and get some sleep during this third night, and I allow myself to be talked into it.

As John drowses off, I go to sleep in the motel that borders the hospital, sure that we will be heading for the rehabilitation center in the morning. But when I return to John's bedside, the breathing tube has been re-inserted. He never regains consciousness.

A day later, all three daughters arrive, but I am still in denial.

Dr. Gillespie gives us the final word, which he actually calls "the speech." Nothing more can be done for John. In the end, his lungs, rather than the "minor" brain injury, will kill my husband. Dr. Gillespie's speech is pathetically vacuous. He assures us that he "knows" that John is a good man, since he can read the sorrow on the faces of those who loved him. It is so obviously canned material that I feel like slapping the man.

Somehow, I still don't believe it. We just had lunch together. He was going to tell me about Willa.

The four of us, his wife and his three daughters, are with him as he draws his last difficult breath. His beautiful long narrow hands are puffed, short, and swollen with the liquid that filled his lungs.

He dies on May 6, 2011. Those last painful breaths will be with me until I draw my own.

My John is "lost and gone forever" like Clementine in the song he used to whistle while in the shower.

He will never again hold my hand in the movies or during airplane landings. He will never again read the *New York Times* as we sit in the coffee shop, and he will never again tell me what he has read in his pages while I wait to tell him about mine. We will never again read the same mysteries and compare our reactions to plot and character. We will not, as we had hoped, visit Lizbet Salender's Stockholm or walk on the beach together. John will never drive me to work or pick me up after work again. He will never grope for my "boobs" in the bathroom as I ineffectually proclaim my right to privacy. He will never again be together with me to complete that "cute old couple that actually talk to each other" role in the various coffee shops and restaurants where the servers frequently commented on our togetherness, while I scorned their intrusions into our privacy.

What a snob I had been! What a fool! How madly I now envy all the old couples I see together! And they are everywhere, in the restaurants, at the movies, at the doctor's office. Do they know what they have? Should I be shouting it at them? Or will they, just like I did, resent me for my intrusion into their happy or unhappy lives? Do all these people love each other like John and I did or do they just tolerate each other's presence? I want so much to scream at them. "Wake up you dopes! Don't you know what you have! Don't you know that life will end and that you will be lonely—so very lonely—among all kinds of people?"

John will never give me that secret smile of recognition as he notices me on the staircase at work. He will also not be there doing our income tax, or for handling our banking, or fix the fire alarm or the locks on our house. He will not take walks with me to downtown Yuma. He will not touch his hip bone to mine as we walk. He will never again travel to conferences with me and help me to set up my presentations. He will not be there at our breakfast, lunch, or dinner table. He will not be there to watch "Meet the Press" on Sunday mornings.

I will not be able to complain to him about everything that goes wrong. I will not be able to share with him all the beautiful things that are right. I will not be able to hear about his adventures with cryo-coolers, his childhood, or his old girlfriends. He will not order books for me or presents for our daughters. I will never again sew on his missing shirt buttons or give him those "in-between" haircuts. He will not be there to tell me that "everything will be all right." I never quite believed him, of course, and heaven knows that things were not always "all right." But at those moments when he said it, I did believe him, and he will never be there to say it again. And, let's face it. Things will never be "all right" again. How can they be "all right" without John?

He will never tell me that bacon is kosher as long as I serve it because I, as a Holocaust survivor, and Jewish mother have special dispensation on such things. He will not be there to talk about the lives of our daughters and their children. He will never again forget dirty coffee cups scattered all through the house. He will never again stroke his wonderful long legs against mine. He will never again tell me about the News of the Jews as they appear in the English version of the Hebrew paper *HaAretz*. He will never again be there to kiss me "Shabbat Shalom" at the end of Friday night services. He will not carry the heavy dishes that I bring to potluck suppers. He will never be there to make every hotel room seem like home that welcomes us for a touch of luxury. He will not be there to share a dreamed-of vacation at the King David Hotel in Jerusalem. He will not be there to explain Algebra to any willing and needing grandchild.

Worst of all, he will not be there in bed next to me—not in the morning and not at night to tell me that he loves me, as I find and kiss the secret places. He will never again be in my arms. How can death be so final? How can we ever grasp the finality?

WHO AM I NOW?

The day after John's death, two of my daughters return to their other lives. Tammy will stay with me to take care of things that must be taken care of.

There is only one Jewish undertaker in Phoenix, Arizona, and he knows all about sending bodies to Israel. We sit across the desk from Mr. Lipsteen, who is clean-shaven and sports a knitted *kipa* (sculcap). He speaks in the pleasantly modulated voice of reasonableness slightly tinged by sorrow. It is a voice appropriate to the profession.

"I am sorry for your loss," he says, as Tammy, who has glanced at the advertisements on his desk notices the menu of interment possibilities listed in a glossy display.

"You provide cremation?" she asks with rising disbelief in her voice. Cremation is, of course, not permitted in traditional Jewish practice, and this man's head covering presumably places him within such religious practice, but this, I know, is multicultural America, and the equanimity in Mr. Lipsteen's voice is clearly unapologetic.

"We cater to all kinds of Jews." His voice wafts with

disapproval as he continues, "So, I understand that you want a secular funeral in Israel. Well, you just better make sure that someone is there to meet the body at Ben Gurion Airport. Body snatching by some of the more religious elements, who insist on a proper religious burial, is not all that uncommon over there."

This is not a problem I had anticipated, and I sit in stunned incredulity, but Tammy understands. She assures me that she has made the necessary provisions. "Don't worry, Mom. Daddy's body will make it to his grave in the secular cemetery of Kiryat Arba."

"Will he need a passport?" I idiotically ask, and Mr. Lipsteen promptly puts me in my place with a condescending look and a wave of dismissal.

I write checks with numbers that are greater than I have ever written. My signature comes out shaky. The sum that John and I had set aside for emergencies is dwindling fast. We have been taught that "Life is always and always will be unpredictable."

As I face Mr. Lipsteen, the future vanishes. The running video tape of my mind has suddenly been cut. Yes, arrangements have to be made. It's business as usual for Mr. Lipsteen and my role here is to accommodate that business—business—the busy-ness of the world—the busy world in which I find myself frozen within an ice block of improbability.

When I was younger, I pictured myself as a successful teacher, possibly married to a rabbi. In the evenings, this future me would be reading student papers, as the imagined rabbi husband worked on his sermons, and our three children peacefully slept under ironed sheets and tucked-in blankets. At least one of those dreamed of children would, of course, be a son whose bar-mitzvah would become one of the culminating moments of our Jewishly embedded lives. My rabbi husband would be a tall, thin, nerd—much like my father.

In real life, I married John Hess and was happily married to him for 53 years. But how on earth does one summarize 53 years? John was not a rabbi. He was a physics major, who had

Jewish parents, but who had been brought up in totally assimilated settings featuring yearly gift exchanges under Christmas trees that were tastefully decorated with white candles. John was indeed tall and thin, but we never worked together in the evenings. I did not understand the physics he was working on, and he was a morning person, while I am a classic night owl. We did have three children, three wonderful daughters.

As a Holocaust survivor, I felt it my duty to bring Jewish children into the world. But neither John nor I knew anything about Judaism. John had been brought up in entirely secular settings, and my Jewish education had been very limited, superficial at best.

The idea of life in Israel had been on my mind since I was five years old and my grandmother had given me an orange imported from Palestine. The irresistible sweetness of that orange symbolized the fulfillment of the two-thousand-year-old dream of return to the Jewish homeland. John read *Exodus* by Leon Uris and then readily joined me in the dream. We would bring up Jewish children who never experienced minority status and who would sense only the emotions of pride and joy connected to their Judaism. We felt that if that two-thousand-year-old waited-for miracle had actually happened in our lifetime, surely we had to participate in it. We saw Israel as a quick and efficient immersion course into living a Jewish life.

At first, we thought of it only as a stay of a few years, but by the end of our first year, John had become totally committed. To be an Israeli is quite different from being a Jew in any land of the dispersion.

In present day America, Jews form a minority that, even when it thrives, lives in a state of perpetual tension between assimilation and guardianship of its enriching uniqueness. It is a condition of cultural anxiety that in its most simplistic form pops up, for example, when a crime that has captured national attention can be traced to a Jewish name, and sigh of communal relief when, no—thank goodness no Jew involved!

In Israel, Jews, particularly of the Askenazi (European) persuasion, readily become cultural WASPS. It is their culture, their language, their literature, their holidays that are the cultural norm. They live a privileged life and as all privileged groups they are entirely unaware of their advantages. They are the fish who have no idea what water is, as they frolic in its embrace.

My daughters grew up in such a favored place, and we felt that in these family plans, as in much else, we had fairly much seen God as our amiable planning companion, and certainly never as that snickering puppeteer.

But nothing had prepared me for becoming a widow. Strangely, this is the first time that I experience genuine grief. It is a peculiar thing to say for someone who is a Holocaust survivor and whose entire family, parents, grandparents, aunts, uncles and cousins were all murdered in Hitler's industrial death complex.

But, you see, these people just vanished from my life. They were gone and I learned to live without them. I taught myself not to think about them. I taught myself to forget. I got to be very good at forgetting.

But I don't want to forget John. I feel that as long as I remember and as long as my grief burns, as long as missing him remains an acute pain, I am somehow still keeping him. I am John's widow. I am Natalie Hess. John has given me his name. I carry his name just as I wear the gold band that he placed on my ring finger on June 20, in 1958.

The wedding ring wasn't easy to remove from John's swollen finger. I wear it on a chain around my neck. I am the widow of John Hess. I am a widow. I am a widow. I am a widow. I am writing the sentence over and over again. Just so that it sticks. Just so that I understand what my social role is now, and how I should deport myself correctly in this new identity.

"Widows and orphans."

The phrase echoes and reverberates. Widows and orphans are the culture's accepted objects of pity. It is always "widows and orphans." It is never "widowers and orphans", of course. Widowers are the beloved bachelors of the social stage. Widowers are the desired ones—fought over by an adoring bevy of ladies who are desperately seeking—seeking refuge in an uncertain world—seeking refuge in the sheltering arms of yet another man—a man to serve, to take to the doctor's office, to make breakfast for, to worry about, to hold hands in the movies with, to kiss for Shabbat Shalom, to be grounded together with in a couple-centered universe.

I read endless chick-lit books for consolation. I find a description of a village scene in Elizabeth Noble's best-selling *The Way We Were* appropriate: "Everyone, it seemed, was dancing. Except for the old widows in black who sat on metal chairs around the edges watching."

Am I ready for that metal chair on the edges? Is my role now that of watcher as life keeps on dancing? Will I have the patience? The forbearance?

In *The King and I*, Anna, the widow, identifies with the world of "young lovers" as she graciously sings "I've had a Love Like You." Somehow that "having had" is supposed to bring a sense of satisfaction. In actuality, it just brings on jealousy and resentment. What right do all these people have to have a love, while my love is so completely and absolutely gone? And let's face it, after 53 years of downs and ups, my love is so much more real than that of those "young lovers." It is so much more sweet and tender. You see, we knew and understood each other's flaws and weaknesses, and yet, in spite of, and maybe even because of, we did love—we loved so much... and life without all that right now seems so meaningless.

My survival strategy has always been to forget. I have forgotten so much. It seemed better to just forget and get on with life. I have forgotten hunger and cold. I have forgotten desertion. I have forgotten humiliation. I have forgotten ambition. But, please, dear God, I don't want to forget John. I don't want to forget anything about him. "Please, please dear God, help me to remember everything."

As long as I have the memories, John is still here with me. So, at this moment, what do I remember about John, whose leftover coffee cups are invariably scattered all over the house? He dreamed about bringing a new cooling system to Yuma. He loved to munch on *Egozi*, the candy bar that still circulates in Israel. He read good night stories to the girls when they were little. He liked *Good Night Moon* and *Mike Mulligan's Steam Shovel*. He was the one who took the girls to see the annual circus. I hated circuses. He took the girls on the climb up to the Masada for their Bat Mitzvah moment. When we first started learning Hebrew, he would put several words together, think of them as one word, and frantically search for the meaning of the non-existent combination. He loved peanut brittle but he had pretty much given up sweets in his later years. He loved to eat lamb chops, and we frequently had those for dinner when we were young, but he effortlessly gave up these cholesterol bombs, as we grew older, and he readily switched to fish. Although, when we went out for a special dinner at Hunter's Restaurant, it was still lamb chops and baked potato for him. Breakfast was his most important meal—pancakes, the Swedish ones at the Pancake House, or French toast, or sunny-side-up eggs with bacon and hash browns. There was always orange juice and good coffee. He taught me the value of good coffee. He stopped smoking overnight, even before I knew him. He claimed that cigarettes made him sick, but I was always amazed how quickly and efficiently he was able to quit all those "unhealthy" habits that the rest of humanity finds so difficult to relinquish. He liked Latte at Starbucks and always ordered the "Grande" size. He liked Boston Cream Pie. He played lots of Solitaire—first the manual version and later on the computer. He had learned the game from his grandmother, Lilian Harris. He always showered and shaved in the morning and was very particular about keeping his razor private. He taught himself thermodynamics, and these books are among those I still keep on my bookshelf. He managed to put together the company "Cryostar" which for some time competed with very big names in the Cryo-cooler world. His needs were simple, but definite. One of his rare anger fits came when early in our marriage I used his razor to shave my legs. Another such fit occurred when a visiting boyfriend of one of our daughters mistakenly made use of the implement.He wrote a beautiful explanation of how to do long division, which he sent to our grandson, Adam, by way of instruction.

I knew about two former girlfriends—Marjorie and Curry. He finished both of those relationships when he found himself too involved emotionally. Evidently neither one of these ladies demanded marriage as I later did. John knew that his parents had brought him to life in the hope that he would cement their unhappy union. He felt burdened by his own lack of success in these matters, and lived in dread of bringing an unwanted child to the world.

John taught both me and our three daughters how to drive. He had cultivated a clear and very legible handwriting. Looking through our well-worn mutual address book, I can spot his clarity among my scribbles. He whistled beautifully, and did so when driving. One of his favorite songs was *She'll be Coming around the Mountain when She Comes*. John loved me fully and completely. I was his person, and he was mine. Much of his world was physics and math—worlds into which I had no entrance, but admired at a respectful distance. I loved John fully and unconditionally and, thank God, I told him so at least three times a day. I never stopped being grateful for our union.

My world without him is very different. I constantly seem to lose my place in it, and I have to accept that he will not be there to find me. In so many ways he is, of course, still with me. I still laugh at the jokes he told me. I still buy radishes because he loved them in his salad. I still explain things to him and ask for his approval. And dear Lord help me, I still hope to see him again in some other modality.

SITTING SHIVA

"*Shiva*," the Hebrew word for seven, is the seven-day mourning period that follows a Jewish funeral. While the funeral itself focuses on the deceased, the Shiva and the 30 days of mourning following it, give attention to the grief of the mourners. During the Shiva, family and those who wish to offer condolences meet at the home of the deceased or the home of one of the mourners. In observant homes, the mirrors are covered to serve as a reminder that human vanity disappears in the face of death, and traditional prayers are recited each day. Guests bring food to free mourners from the obligations of hosting. In Israel, even among the least observant, Shiva visits are common, expected, and seen as obligatory.

"You can miss someone's wedding or a baby's *Brit* (the circumcision ceremony), but don't miss the Shiva," a friend once advised me. "People remember who has visited during the Shiva, so please go. Even if you were not all that close to the mourner or to the deceased, go. You can't be wrong by attending. You can be very wrong by not showing up."

When visiting a Shiva, one can talk about the departed, but one can actually talk about anything. The idea is that you have come; that you have offered condolences and concern; that you have shared in communal understanding of the gravity of death as a life-changing event and that you are acknowledging a moment of human inevitability.

One of our daughters had placed death announcements in the English Language *Jerusalem Post* and in the Hebrew *HaAretz*. We hold the Shiva at my youngest daughter's home in Mevaseret Zion. I had always felt that John and I lived very private lives—especially during our 24 years in Israel where our family of five often seemed to be on a raft held tightly together as we floated in unfamiliar waters. So, I must say that I am surprised at the unexpectedly large attendance both at the funeral and at the Shiva. We had, after all, already been away for more than 20 years.

Who would remember us? I wondered.

Evidently, a great many people did. Israel is a small country. People stay in place. I had taught English in a central Jerusalem high school. Former students still remembered me, so did former colleagues, and the young teachers I had trained. Many of John's former colleagues from the Hebrew University came. John's niece, who happened to be on a trip to Israel came. David Webster, a nephew from Massachusetts, came especially for the occasion. Two of my foster-brothers from Sweden came with their wives. Gösta, the older brother, had recently undergone a back operation. He was still on crutches and suffered back pain. Yet, astonishingly, he felt the need to come.

"Of course, we had to come; of course we had to come!" he reiterated as I expressed my wonder and appreciation.

People whom we had met and befriended on the Shalom Boat when we first came to Israel in 1964 showed up. Two of our three daughters had created their own lives in Israel and their friends and colleagues came in droves. It was wall-to-wall people for seven full days.

The days started at 7:00 in the morning when those who

wanted to call before work arrived, and the days would end just before midnight, when we finished the last load of dishwashing, vacuumed, and swept. My in-laws kept bringing in wonderfully aromatic homemade dishes and whenever the food supply seemed to run short, Ronen, my son-in-law, made a quick trip to Abu Ghosh, the nearby Arab village, and soon the house was again submerged in gastronomic bouquets. Throughout all this, I pretty much function as a poorly designed robot. Time seems curiously flat.

Where is John? I kept asking myself and doing an internal shudder, as I once more explained to myself that John is gone.

No, I sternly told myself. *No, he is not in the bathroom; no, he has not gone on one of his solitary walks. No, he is not out there in search for a non-existent Starbucks. In the midst of this huge social extravaganza, he has abandoned me. He is gone.*

Of course, I reminded myself, *John was always terribly uncomfortable on these social occasions. This one, thank goodness, he can sit out, and just be an observer, as I do the chatting. And I sure don't feel like doing the chatting.*

Still, I make endless small talk. Or, rather, I listen to endless small talk. I hear about the marvellous grandchildren, about the last person fired, about a knitted scarf, about how the previous fatty got it all off through the last Weight Watcher scheme, and about several avoided heart attacks. I am told which organizations to join and which to stay away from. I am told that President Obama "is not a Zionist," and I am reminded that Hillary Clinton had given Suha Arafat a hug. I am told about foolish money schemes—that one I try to pay close attention to.

Come on, Natalie, I tell myself. *You are a widow now. Get on the stick. If nothing else, you must start thinking about your financial future.* But, my brain is totally unplugged and maybe that is the real function of a Shiva—to let both the brain and the emotional systems, chances to unplug.

Two people seem to return for more than one visit. One is

Birgit, whom I knew in Sweden. Birgit belongs to one of the older Jewish families in Sweden—the "Mayflower Jews" of Sweden. I had, of course, been a Holocaust survivor-immigrant newcomer, the "wretched refuse" lot translated to Swedish, and, of course, I had envied those long-ago pre-war arrivals. They seemed so at home. Were they really? Probably not—they weren't very tall and blond anyway—that would take a few more generations.

Birgit is now a tourist guide in Israel. She tells me that she loves her job, and she encourages me to join an organization of Swedish women who live abroad. I had always been ill at ease around those established, well-to-do Swedish "Mayflowernicks," and that sensation of outsiderness returns and wraps me in discomfort, as I chat with Birgit in a mixture of Swedish and Hebrew. I ask her to tell me what she likes about being a guide. Her answer is long and enthusiastic and allows me to fade away.

The other person who seems to appear more than once is a small man by the name of Fredrick Cohen. He speaks both English and Hebrew with a German accent and tells me that I had taught his son Yoav, who is now a successful engineer.

"You saved Yoav, you know," he explains. "If it weren't for you, he might have dropped out of high school."

I do remember Yoav—a very nice kid, not really in need of anyone's special attention.

Fredrick tells me that tough times are ahead for me. "Nothing will ever be the same, so don't even try to be the person you used to be. But, believe it or not, things do get easier. Eventually, you'll learn to be your own best friend. You'll learn to look out for yourself. You'll even learn how to enjoy life. It's not the same, never the same, but you'll re-discover yourself. You'll start doing new things. Having new thoughts. Remember what I tell you. Things do get easier."

I hear what he says through a fog of misunderstanding and curious indifference. He tells me about the elegant assisted living facility where he now resides and invites me to visit. I promise to do so with every intention of forgetting all about it.

Sometime during day five, I stand in the upstairs bathroom unable to open the door. I push the door. I fiddle with the lock. I can't open it. I find a pair of scissors and work the lock with them. Nothing. I am clearly trapped. Mortification strikes. I re-flush the toilet, considering my options—to shout or not to shout, to bang on the door or not. "Come on girl, be grown up!"

I imagine the turmoil downstairs. "Where is mother? Why hasn't someone looked out for her? Where is that banging coming from? Is she sick up there?"

I look in the mirror, the one that has not been covered, and stare at my reflection. Who is that dreadful-looking old woman staring back at me? She seems to have lost half of her hair and what is left is so much more leaden gray. There are huge deeply embedded creases on both sides of her face. When did that happen? The eyes, that had always been her best feature, seem to have shrunk and yellowed. Is this a woman who can be saved? How can she possibly cope alone? There is a handy grave waiting for her so close by. It would be such a relief to just sit down and let things go —softly and peacefully—not to cause any bother—not to trouble anyone—just to fade away. I try to smile at the woman in the mirror. The image grins mirthlessly back.

Just put out the light, I tell myself. That's what John always said. That's what he said when the kitchen was full of dirty dishes. "Just put out the light. Click! See how easy it is!"

And then, I would, of course, turn it back on and do the dishes. The dishes had to be done. So much always had to be done. Why not just kiss and cuddle? Why not be aware of what you have? Why does it have to be gone before you know and feel its magic? Why must you lose it before you know what you had?

Here in the bathroom without John, I do put out the light. There is no window in the bathroom. The darkness is black and deep. The horrible woman in the mirror vanishes, and I wish so much that I could cry.

Then, for some unexplainable reason, the darkness feels velvety and liberating. I think about the door, but somehow, I cannot be bothered. Of course, I will bang on the door. Of course, there will be a racket. Of course, someone will come up and get me out. Of course, I will feel awkward and idiotic, but really who cares? Everyone has his or her own troubles. Mine are just another tiny pinch of bitterness in the soup of human-tragedy. But for a while, I savor the velvety blackness and smell the perfume of left-out after-shave.

From downstairs, comes the soft murmur of socialization.

Hey, I am not the only old widow in the world. People make the best of things. So will I. I have great daughters. I have wonderful grandchildren. There is much to be grateful for, I tell myself. Glass half full and all that! If you hang around feeling so sorry for yourself, why should anyone ever want to be near you? You don't have John who will put up with all your moods and think you are wonderful anyway. Think of that, My Lady Sorrowful. Eventually, you should be able to cry, but please not in public, kindly never in public. Paint a proper smile on your face, girl. Keep the ball rolling. Hey, you are still a mom, a grandma. Your job still is to set a good example. That game isn't over until it's over, and if you continue as a sourpuss, they will mostly just be glad to have you out of the way—think of that, Lady Sorrowful. Think of that! That's right, things can always get worse! A lot worse!

I try the door one more time and, incredibly, it just opens. Open Sesame! May it stay open!

At the conclusion of the Shiva, we follow tradition with a visit to the gravesite. There is a place reserved for me right next to John's. I have paid for it. Paid dearly—probably overpaid. Once more, I wonder how long it will take me to get there. I could plan things better if I just knew how much time I had left. I know that I have already made some wrong decisions, and I know that there are many more decisions to be made. But right now I don't want to think about them. I use the old Scarlet O'Hara trick. "I will think about it tomorrow." I open the prayer book and gratefully sink into the prayers that tradition has placed before me.

"Mommy," says my youngest daughter as we walk away from the cemetery, "you know that Fredrick Cohen? He really likes you. I know that you are not the least bit interested, but I thought that I would tell you, anyway. I thought that it might be a morale booster for you."

I give her a dismissive look, but as we drive home, it dawns on me. I really am a single woman again. How very weird. The last time I was a single woman, I was 21 years old, a single woman on the marriage market—that dismal place where antennae of loneliness stretch out in search of reception. How strange! How very bizarre! I would think about it tomorrow.

MORNING WALKS IN MEVASERET ZION

I stay in Israel for a month after the Shiva, spending part of my time in Haifa with Debby and part in Mevaseret Zion, a suburb of Jerusalem, where Tammy lives.

Mevaseret Zion is located on a mountain ridge between Tel Aviv and Jerusalem. The place has an impressive history that stretches from the Roman occupation of Judea through the Crusader period, the Arab settlement, the British Mandate, and into the present state of Israel. The neighborhood looks up to a mountaintop where the crusaders built a castle. One can still see this castle from many vantage points. The ghosts that live there have certainly been privileged to observe the evolution of an interesting historical panorama. Tammy and her husband, Ronen, are renting the house where they now live because the schools in the district have a good reputation. Behind their home is a great, largely uninhabited valley full of paths created by both people and animals.

My present state of restlessness and sleeplessness gets me out early in the morning for walks in the valley. The walks burn off some of my agitation and anxiety, but unfortunately, I often get lost, and make many wrong turns before finding my way back. Mornings these days are difficult. Sleep is drug-induced, fitful at best, and filled with dreams of apprehension. I sleep about five hours a night and wake up expecting John to be next to me, but next to me is Ayelet, my granddaughter, who is still sleeping soundly. She falls asleep next to me every night as soon as I have finished two of her requested stories. *Clifford, the Big Red Dog*, is a perennial favorite. So is, *Olivia, the Great Mouse Detective*.

I eat a couple of crackers and swallow one half of the Paxil that Ronen, who is a psychiatrist, has prescribed for me. Then begins the struggle to find my sneakers. Where have they gone to now? Why aren't they under the bed where I clearly remember parking them last night? Eventually, I find them in the closet. If I can only get up quietly not to wake anyone in the house and get out for a walk, maybe the fretfulness will go away.

I make my way carefully down the stairs. Tammy is already up. She is at the kitchen table, busy with her computer. She is desperately trying to finish the chapter of a book that has to be completed to be included in her tenure application. Sometimes she chucks it all and joins me for the morning walk. At other more focused times, like this morning, she lets me go on my own.

The walk leads me behind the house in a circle that encompasses the lower portion of Mevaseret Zion. The valley is rich in vegetation, which, like the population of Israel, has gradually migrated from everywhere in the world to form a cohesive whole. It is a landscape that appeases me and helps me to move into the semblance of daily functioning tranquility. I pass fir trees of a distinctly European feel, undoubtedly planted there by the Keren Kayemeth (Jewish Fund for Restoration) together with *Sabra* cacti, eucalyptus, dill, and the succulent native Weavers. The dill reaching across my path is yellow lace.

Some days I fast-walk, nervously examining my stumbling feet, and feeling grateful that the ups and downs of the terrain allow me to distribute my nervous energy; at other times, I walk slowly and let the fusion of dry thistles, succulent tamarisks, the occasional cedar tree together with all those lacily embracing dill formations capture my soul and encase me in comforting wonder. The smell of dill is piquant and a bit peppery. Birds make patterns across a cloudless June sky and I feel John's presence. He would have followed me out, not wanting me to be alone on my own in this unknown territory. I wonder if I will ever be able to stop missing him.

This morning I am on my own. I am glad. I would not have been able to keep up with Tammy's brisk pace today. I feel old, weak, and disoriented. Did I take the right turn at the crest of that hill?

Suddenly there are voices shouting in Arabic. Two pick-up trucks block my path. Six men are busily unloading a variety of chainsaws, scythes and axes. As they unload, I am clearly aware of the deadly razor-sharpness of all their equipment. Everything looks menacing. The sharp scythes are clearly guillotines.

The path in front of me allows me only one direction. I will have to pass them. There is no way around them unless I am willing to be totally scratched up by thorny cacti on my right, or ready to fall off a cliff on my left.

Do these guys have an urge to cut my head off? A peaceful old Jewish lady taking her morning walk? Shouldn't I be minding the grandbabies? Am I just a Jewish *sharmuta*,[1] wandering about like no decent woman should? Wouldn't it be just as well to cut her throat considering all that handy equipment that could certainly do the job? Who would know? Who could care? It would be a good lesson for all decent womanhood to get rid of her.

"*Sabbah-el-her*[2]" I try to shout. My voice comes out like a whiny squeak.

They don't answer with the standard response. They stand in double rows—three on each side as I pass by them and around the pickup. Their eyes are blank. They seem to look at me with open-eyed non-communicative animosity. My knees are weak. My

185

mouth is dry. My stomach is screaming. I am scared to death. As soon as I have passed them, I pick up speed like mad. My knees hurt, but I break into a run. Sweat is running down my forehead. This is silly. I slow my pace. High up on my right, I begin to see family homes. Suddenly there are dog-walkers. A woman walks by at a jaunty pace. I stop to pet the dog.

"*Boker Tov*[3]" she tells me. Never has Hebrew sounded so rich and melodious.

"*Boker or*[4]" I answer, and my voice sounds fairly close to normal. Where am I? Oh, there is the turn in the road that I know, and there is that old rusty gate, and just a short climb ahead is the civilized road that leads to my daughter's house.

Tammy has made breakfast. The kids are up! Ayelet wants French toast. Rachel prefers scrambled eggs. There is spilled cereal and milk to be wiped up. The rabbits have gotten out of their cage. The living room needs to be swept. Ronen offers advice on a school project.

"There were some Arabs on the road below," I tell Tammy.

"Yes," she says and her voice is noncommittally morning casual. "They are clearing the paths. It's some security issue. They come early, so they can go to their other, real jobs later."

I eat my yogurt in contemplative appreciation. To my daughter, the permanent resident of Mevaseret, my imagined attackers are just ordinary folks going about their customary job, trying to make a bit of extra cash to supplement meager incomes and support families.

Why had it been so clear to me that they were out to get me? Why did fear grasp and tangle my innards, each time I heard Arabic shouted? And yet she had ever so offhandedly, brought in the "security issue."

"Some security issue," she had blithely said. "Some security issue," that blessed euphemism which includes terrorism, blood baths, bereavement, pogrom and piety—ah yes—those insignificant "security issues"—just a part of life—what else—security issues.

And there they had been. Arabs just doing an early morning job to increase their income just a bit; to buy an extra pair of shoes for a kid, a shawl for the wife; meat for the Ramadan's evening meal.

No wonder it was annoying to stop work, even for a couple of minutes, so that an old Jewish lady could cross their path? Where was the menace? What on earth was wrong with me? What had I been thinking? They were clearing the paths. Security—security for whom? For what? For my grandchildren? For theirs? A security issue? Whose security? Their cousin's? My police's? The next suicide bomber's? Perhaps nobody's. Perhaps simply wider paths for the dog-walkers and me. Life would go on. I could eat my yogurt. Just an average day, an ordinary security issue in the daily morning life of the Middle East.

THE IMPROBABLE RICHARD

What can I tell you about Richard? He is a tall scraggly fellow in his early 60s. His graying hair is abundant and unkempt. He is often furious, and he turns red on those occasions. His nose tends to turn purple. He likes flashy ties and fancy silver belt buckles.

Was it just a coincidence that his house was flooded on the very same night that John died? Was it a coincidence that exactly when I desperately needed someone to help me with the dreadful bureaucracy of our lives, Richard, the master of officialdom and the king of decoding bureaucratic demands and translating *officialeeze* into plain English made his appearance and became not only my angel of orderliness but also the house sitter that I so badly needed? Was it just mutual loss and mutual need that brought Richard and me together?

I don't believe that it happened that way. Instead, I believe that when John arrived before his maker, he realized the mess he had left me in. Knowing my propensities or lack thereof, he invoked the privileges due only to the righteous and insisted that the creator make some provisions. This is why I sometimes truly believe that a higher power sent Richard to me in my hour of need. You should know that I am an absolute dunce when it comes to administrative issues of any kind. I am practically allergic to them. John handled all that—by that, I mean leases of all varieties, contracts, taxes, insurances, and all financial or clerical aspects of our lives. I made a decent salary. It went into our mutual account and John handled it. I just wasn't interested, and John did a good job, as far as I was concerned, which meant that I never thought about these things.Our system of forms was more or less alphabetically arranged in several filing cabinets as well as in many scattered folders about the house. I didn't have to think about these things, and I did my best not to. My job was to manage our social obligations, which I did reasonably well. The system had worked for us nicely for 53 years. John and I matched each other's neuroses quite perfectly.

So how does Richard fit into all this? He was the only person in the small Jewish congregation of Yuma, Arizona whom I thoroughly disliked. That, of course, was all before he became my guardian angel.

When John and I first arrived in Yuma, we decided to join the only Jewish gig in town, the Reform congregation, which consisted of about 35 families. Student rabbis from Los Angeles serviced us. They were generally bright young people, who on Fridays brought us what they had learned on Thursdays. Our Friday night services were lively and interesting, a far cry from the stilted classical Reform, which I had known in Evansville, Indiana during the fifties. Our Saturday morning Torah studies brought us together for spirited discussion. We were less contentious with one another than most Jewish groups—not because we were less opinionated, but simply because we didn't have that "other synagogue" to escape to. It was a close-knit group that gradually began to feel like an extended family. I served as its secretary. John, for some time, was the treasurer. John and I did our Bar/Bat mitzvah ceremonies with an adult group. I felt very close to most members. The little congregation gave me a sense of belonging that I had never previously experienced.

Richard Ivens and his wife Susan were members too. Susan, a nurse, is not Jewish. It was generally accepted that she was an angel of patience and forbearance. Otherwise, how could she possibly put up with Richard? He was known for his bad temper, his irritability, and his not infrequent outbursts of anger. To me, he seemed brash and perpetually out of sorts. When he was not fuming, he was annoyed or annoying. Richard owned and operated a used car lot, and when we mistakenly called him up on a Sunday, to inquire about a car, he blew his stack: "You call me about business on Sunday!" he roared.

I couldn't resist reminding him that Sunday really was not his Sabbath. Needless to say, we bought our car elsewhere.

One never knew when Richard might burst out from a subterranean explosion. I thought it best to be polite and keep my distance. John, however, always liked Richard. I could never understand how or why. I wasn't there during those board meetings, but members of the congregation reported that Richard had regularly and consistently abused John, who served the board as treasurer.

As I told you, I usually stayed away from Richard, but once I actually screamed at him. That particular incident occurred when he insisted that an article about the life of our little congregation be published on the front page of the local newspaper. The time was right before the Jewish High Holidays. Richard wanted the greater Yuma community to know about us. He hoped for community participation. In his way of thinking, the general community was, no doubt, curious about what Jews did during their High Holiday services, and he wanted us on display.

I, on the other hand, represented those of us who were frightened by such exposure. I saw such blatant revelation as a security risk. One never knew about nut cases. It was true that nothing of *"that kind"* had ever happened in Yuma, but I knew that one could never tell about these things. It's not that I wanted to hide. Everyone knew that I was Jewish.

I certainly did not want our congregational doors locked, but positioning us on the front page, looked to me like asking for trouble. I knew from personal encounters that there was plenty of anti-Semitism lurking both in Arizona and in Yuma. On the steps of Northern Arizona University—Yuma branch campus, I had seen young bodies sporting tattoos of a swastika—occasionally on unmistakably Mexican bodies, Mexican immigrant bodies. What were these kids thinking? Did they understand how they were defacing themselves? Well, I wasn't the person who would tell them.

Richard and I had unpleasant conversations. He called me paranoid. I called him ridiculous. I felt bad about the whole thing. It disturbs me when people "kindly understand my fears." I am permitted to have such fears since I am a Holocaust survivor. I may be paranoid, but real dangers do exist, and I see no reason to court them. At home, I would fret and fume about Richard, but John always defended him.

"He is a good sort," John would say. "He is a real brick! He works hard for the congregation."

I have to admit that I didn't like the feeling of animosity that existed between Richard and me. It soured the sense of pleasure and belonging that I felt as a member of our little congregation. So, before Yom Kippur[1] of 2010 I decided to do the right thing. Tradition demands that prior to Yom Kippur we are to ask forgiveness of anyone we might have offended during the year. I decided to call Richard and apologize. It wasn't easy, but I gritted my teeth and made the call, and I felt a load lifted when Richard graciously accepted my plea. Well that was that! The gesture did not erase my sense of ill feeling whenever I faced Richard, but it did allow me to continue my satisfying congregational life.

This, of course, all happened before John died. John died on

May the 6, 2011. On May the 7, two of my daughters returned to their other lives.

When it comes to existential angst, I have noticed that in spite of cultural differences and political orientations, there seem to be two kinds of belief systems that guide humanity. One such system promotes an overriding plan that has organized and continues to take an interest in the universe—an intelligence that we cannot fathom or grasp, but which involves both our individual and our social destinies. Those who espouse this basic conviction may talk about it in religious or philosophical terms, but the thought that meaning beyond our comprehension exists gives them comfort in what often appears to be an incomprehensible and disturbing universe. The second view positions total distrust in anything beyond known reality and comprehension. Human existence and the survival of the world are, according to such a vision, merely products of a cosmic accident in which events happen without rhyme or reason, and in which our lives are simply those of living organisms, who must make the best of things at the top of a food chain.

I probably lean toward the first group. I find membership in the second too depressing and too heartbreaking for survival. It's not the kind of world I want to live in, and so I don't. I am giving you the above as background to what happened between Richard and me on the day after John died. If I had, at the time, belonged to the second group, I might write off what occurred as just a coincidence. But I have heard from proponents in my group that "there are really no coincidences." Do I absolutely accept such a point of view? Not really, not every day, not every hour, but in the case of Richard, I tend to hedge my bets. You can, if you so wish, consider me misguided, superstitious or grasping at straws. The author, Joan Didion would, no doubt, view me as another victim of "magical thinking" that belongs in the sorrows of first-year widowhood.[2] I will let you be the judge.

The night my daughter and I returned to Yuma, I spent all my time paying bills and straightening out papers that had accumulated during the two weeks I had spent in the hospital with John. The following morning, we were to catch a plane on our way to Israel via New York City. In the evening, Richard came to visit us. The visit was cordial but quite formal. Richard explained that he had dealt professionally with grieving families and that he had just recently closed his own father's affairs. "That was a nightmare!"

He kindly offered his service, with the usual, "feel free to count on me if you need anything." Of course, I had heard this sentence repeated both in speech and in writing. I wonder how many times I, too, had made such an offer, never thinking that anyone would take me up on it, just as I certainly didn't intend to burden anyone. I thanked Richard politely and pretended to be impressed by, what I considered his rather superficial advice:

"Make sure that you call social security." (I had.)

"Contact life insurance agencies." (I had.)

"Contact your car insurance." (I had.)

"Be sure that someone gets your mail while you are away" (I had actually spoken to Mary Welter, my next-door neighbor, but I seriously worried about that aspect. It was so easy for mail to get lost.)

"When in doubt, use the 'widow card.'" (That was a new one for me.) What did he mean? Well, I would soon find out.

As I accompanied Richard to the door, I decided to erase my worries until the funeral and Shiva were over. At the door, Richard and I were subdued and stuck to the formulaically frozen performance that we had agreed was appropriate for the relationship. And I must admit that I was touched by his obvious attempt to be helpful, but I had much to do and was glad to see him go.

Two hours later, when I was still immersed in paper work, he called and everything had changed. It was a very different Richard on the phone. His voice was shaking when he talked. "You aren't going to believe this, Natalie. My house is completely flooded. I am walking around with water up to my knees. Furniture and clothes are ruined. Thank God, Susan is in Washington with the grandkids. My insurance doesn't answer. I don't know what I am doing."

"Come over, again," was all I could think to say.

Richard came, and suddenly we were both talking like mad.

"Where did the water come from?"

"I don't know. I couldn't find a broken pipe anywhere."

"Did you call the police? The fire department?"

"No one is answering the phone."

"Of course not. It's late, you know. But please call them again in the morning."

We were together in a bundle of anxiety. Richard had nowhere to sleep that night. It didn't take long for us to understand that my home was his for the foreseeable future. We were going to do a *mitzvah* (that curious word that means both good deed and commandment) for each other. Richard and Susan would become my house sitters while I was in Israel for John's funeral and the Shiva. Actually it turned into a much longer stay as my son-in-law, the psychiatrist, soothed me with both knowledge and medication.

When I returned in early September, I was faced with mountains of papers. John did not believe in throwing things away and going through 53 years or so of paper work would have had me quickly committed. The reason I could still think more or less logically was because Richard was there. He, it turned out, is a natural paper person, who can quickly sort papers to be kept, to be chucked, and to be shredded.

Richard knew where on official papers the date appeared and how it should be treated. Richard found the life insurance forms and helped me to fill out the claim forms and get those into the mail. Richard helped to make endless phone calls to sleepy and indifferent clerks. Richard labeled and sorted. In the meanwhile, Susan, the professional nurse, held my hand as my heart pounded, as I paced the floor, and as my anxiety catapulted. Susan cooked and invited me to dinners, which I otherwise would not have eaten. I don't know what I would have done without them because in addition to all the emotional angst, I was tossed into the administrative facet of John's world. An aspect that I had assiduously avoided during our entire marriage. I had been so completely certain that I would be the one to leave this world before John did. I had made many provisions for him on my salary, but I had no idea of what he had done for me, and if it were not for Richard's help, I might not ever have known.

Going through all those papers together with Richard, made me appreciate the relationship that had existed between him and John. Richard looked at the papers with eyes that observed what I might easily have missed. He understood and admired John's work. He was astonished with the patent rights that John had been awarded, the presentations of calculus that John had created, the various business plans that he had attempted, and Richard would burst out with, "Oh John! Good for you John! Aren't you something, John!"

These were the moments when I loved Richard and when I was deeply grateful for his presence. I learned many things about both Richard and Susan. Susan was an observant Catholic while Richard, of course, was a practicing Jew. They managed a gracious practice of both religions. Before each meal the Hebrew blessing over bread was followed by the Catholic benediction. During the Jewish-American "December-Dilemma," when most Jews flee to Chinese restaurants for companionship, Richard and Susan celebrate in an Ecumenical setting with both Menorah and Christmas tree. I learned about Richard and Susan's pride in their adopted African-American grandson and about Richard's enormous contributions to the town's amateur theatricals. I learned that Richard's occasional outbursts of temper were the opposite of John's need to take naps during crucial encounters. Both however signaled lapses—one outward, the other inward in coping mechanisms. Both Susan and I had learned how to live with these and appreciate the real person beneath the inappropriate displays. And yes, Richard's insurance came to the rescue and their home was rebuilt.

Did John send me Richard and Susan? Please God, I cannot help but believe so. I can hear a frantic John approaching the throne and anxiously explaining to the powers that his Nanna would simply go crazy trying to find her way among the papers and that some arrangements had to be made before he could comply with whatever was now expected of him.

In Yuma, I have never heard of water damage to the extent of that which occurred for Richard and Susan. Yuma is in the desert— huge water damage somehow doesn't really fit—even when it comes from suddenly broken pipes. Magical thinking? Not for me, my darling. I know that you are still there. You were there when I walked in the Jerusalem hills. You were there when the magical light of Jerusalem evenings soothed me. You were there when I said *Kadish* on Friday nights and you were there when I wrote in the National Library of the Hebrew University Campus. I could have just walked over to the Physics Department where you used to work and where I used to pick you up in the evenings and sometimes for lunch, but they fired you and you never visited again, so I won't go over, even though I know that if I found someone who knew you, they would no doubt be kind and sympathetic. Death does that for us. It suddenly makes those profoundly important moments of life seem trivial and at the same time unbearably beautiful.

I have moved to Philadelphia now, my darling, and it is winter —a very mild one they tell me. I am, however, learning to wear socks again. Richard continued to look after the house until I managed to sell it, and he has never blown his stack at me, and if he wants to shine on the front pages of the Yuma newspaper, I will even go back there and pose with him. He is a real brick! Just as you always told me.

PART 6

LIFE IN PHILADELPHIA. FINDING CONTENTMENT

HAPPY NEW YEAR!

December, 2013, New Year's Eve. Two and a half years have gone by since John died. The view from my fourteenth-floor apartment in Center City is spectacular. Sitting at the window with my morning coffee, I sense the city life vibrating from below. In an urban environment, there is constant human presence. It hums and makes its way upward to my fourteenth floor. It keeps loneliness at bay. On my left, I can see the Doric columns of the Franklin Institute. The equally impressive city central library is straight ahead. Farther to the right, is a dome shape, which I recognize as the huge helium balloon of the Philadelphia Zoo.

John had once gone up in the balloon with our grandson, David. My fear of heights had kept me firmly grounded. Still I had felt part of the excitement. Hey, those also serve, who only stand and wave. A triumph is not a triumph unless recognized. If I lean forward a bit, I see pedestrians on Arch Street. I study their dress to gauge the temperature of the day. Do I need my down-filled, rainproof winter coat, or will a warm jacket do? Both models are in evidence on Arch Street. My cell phone tells me that the temperature out there is 32 Fahrenheit. I choose my down-filled coat. Better to be a bit too warm than to be freezing. I do have to leave now to keep my doctor's appointment.

Resentfully, I abandon my view. I know that I will be losing it soon. A huge skyscraper is being constructed directly in front of my windows, each story rising menacingly upward to rob me of the ownership I now claim to this my morning's caffeine panorama.

Ah, well, the inside world of my new home is cozy. It is a miniature version of all the homes John and I shared in various places during our 53 years of marriage. His favorite chair is here. The paintings he brought to our union in 1958 have all found places on these new walls. The rounded walrus that invariably adorned his desk is here too, so are many of his physics books. It is hard to believe that two and a half years really have gone by since he died. Were he to walk in the door, as I often imagine him doing, he would feel right at home. I somehow still cannot imagine a real home without him. But this very pleasant place is now my very own home. I have a spacious living room that also serves as a dining room, a nicely appointed kitchen, a bedroom, an office that doubles as guest room, and two bathrooms. In today's complicated world filled with homeless and fleeing refugees all over the globe, this snug and inviting place of books, plants, and pictures seems obscenely extravagant for one person still determined to play house. During our 53-year history together, we lived well, even as a family of five, in smaller and less luxuriant accommodations, so I am well aware of my privileged urban tenancy.

Perhaps I don't exactly live the life of élan, but I have made new friends, among them one of the male persuasion. Actually, I have probably never been quite as "normal" in my life as I now seem to have become. Older Jewish widows abound in Philadelphia, and I am part of that sisterhood. Some of them would have preferred New York, but economic considerations made Philly their good second choice. Many actually live in my co-op. Several attend the courses I take at OLLI (Osher Lifelong Learning

Center). Some work together with me as docents at the Museum of American Jewish History.

Among these are women in whom I recognize the passion that we share for the stories reflected in the material we represent at the museum. Many also populate my book club, and are pleased to join me for dinner, for brunch, or for occasional coffee-with-schmooze and girlfriend communion. It's an honest-to-God sisterhood, a better sorority than the Chi Omega that I belonged to at Indiana State Teachers College all those years ago. Things seem more honest in old age. The wrinkles are there for all to see, and if one wants advice for or against Botox, it is given without reservation. There is also open discussion regarding all sorts of medical functions, warnings, emergencies, and thinning hair. There is lots of sex talk—amazing how raunchy and funny these ladies can get. Nevertheless, there does seem to be a certain depth, even in our frivolous deliberations. The only thing to be avoided is unkindness. This I can live with! Perhaps these really are "the bonus" years, so often hailed in "elder-chick" lit.

"Good bye home," I say as I lock my door and kiss the Jerusalem Mezuzah in its leaning position on my doorpost. The ritual soothes my soul.

The appointment for my annual checkup with the wonderful Dr. Carol Rose Fleischman in Radnor is at 2:30. I am surprised that she made an appointment for New Year's Eve, but I am glad that I got an appointment at all. She has such an overbooked schedule. I have checked with SEPTA (The Pennsylvania department of public transportation) for the most appropriate train times. A train that leaves at 1:19 at the 30th Street Railroad Station in Philadelphia is scheduled to arrive in Radnor 2:10. That should give me plenty of time. I was there a year ago, and discovered, much to my joy, that Penn Medicine, where the Dr. Fleischman plies her trade, is right across the street from the railroad station in Radnor.

I leave my city home for a brisk ten-minute walk to the 30th Street railroad station, a place that, in my mind, is a whole miniature city, or, as one of the colleagues, in the writing class once described it, "a temple to train transportation." The place with its marble floors, its columns, its statuary, its mind-bogglingly high ceilings, and above all, its incessantly pulsating motion in full-of-go-commercial life overtakes me with a combination of wonder, belonging, and at the same time, curious observer detachment.

It's a pleasant half-hour ride to Radnor. The wheels sing lullabies. I close my eyes and almost miss my station. The conductor gallantly offers a hand as I step down from the train—old lady privilege—one might as well take them when and where they show up —heaven knows, that this interesting stage offers few enough advantages. I give the conductor my rescued-princess smile. He reciprocates and salutes in his knight-in-shining-armor character. We all live our stories.

I was here a year ago, and I clearly remember the brick building of Penn Medicine distinctly across the street from the station, but now as I exit the station I don't see them anywhere. Where have they gone? The road in front of me is full of speeding traffic—all, no doubt headed for New Year's Eve at home. Everything else is empty. No stores, no restaurants, and no people.

I was the only one who got off the train. There aren't even any parked cars. No signs of human existence. No traffic light. Speeding cars keep me from crossing the road. I turn to the right and walk around the railroad station, which seems to be in the middle of some sort of a park. I wander here and there. I cross some streets. The suburban houses on their raised hills look like imposing and impenetrable castles. The geography of my surroundings becomes more complex as I continue to meander. Nothing looks familiar. Now I can't even see the railroad station any longer.

Let's face it. I am lost. It is now 2:20. Panic swells in the pit of my stomach and quickly conquers the remaining body parts. Is this how Alzheimer's begins? After all, I was here last year, and I did see those building just as I got out of the railroad station. Have I imagined all that?

"Come on girl; get a grip; get your act together. You are not lost in China. You speak the local lingo and there are family houses all over the place. You just have to get to one, knock on the door and ask for directions." I say all this rather sternly to myself, but I know very well that I am not going to go up any of those well-protected hills and knock on any of those forbidding doors. The entrances are probably somewhere in the back anyway for the likes of me, and how will I locate that entrance? If and when I do, there, no doubt, will be flocks of determined and ferocious dogs guarding these magnificent suburban dwellings. And how am I going to deal with that?

I spot him crossing over two streets away. He is walking toward me. He is a big man wearing something that looks like an official yellow vest. On his head is a brimmed cap tilted forward over his forehead. Advancing towards me, he seems to grow larger with each step. He and I are the only humans in sight in Radnor, Pennsylvania on this street here on New Year's Eve, 2013. When he is only half a block away, I see his unsmiling face formed into a business-like no-nonsense expression. The arms hanging to his sides are huge and menacing. These are hands that could choke. These are hands that could strike. My anxiety reaches boiling point, but I stand still waiting for his arrival. I've got to take my chances. This could be the possible foe or the guardian angel. If he is the villain, then I am clearly the mark—little old lady, carrying a big bag—fodder for any and all destructive instincts.

He, however, is so absorbed in his thoughts that I have to reach out to touch him before he seems to be aware of me. My voice is squeaky when I somehow manage get the question out of my mouth, but he doesn't seem to notice.

"Penn Medicine? Yes, ma'am, right over there by the railroad station. Did you park your car there?"

"No, I came on the train."

"Ah, well, you should have gone through the tunnel to the other side."

He is going that way, anyway. He offers to show me, and we trudge along through the slippery streets and the half-melted yet dangerously intruding piles of snow. My feet are already soaked.

And there we are. Steps lead into the tunnel. The entrance is a dark cavern. From the top of the stairs, the tunnel looks dimly lit, low and endless. The odor of moldy moisture fills my nostrils. He gestures me to move ahead of him. The steps are deep and slippery. I take them cautiously one at a time clutching the railing as I move ahead and allowing both feet to come together before I attempt the next step. My companion's shadow looms hugely over mine. I glance back and see that as we inch into the tunnel, he has to lower his head to avoid touching the ceiling. There are no other people around, and I, as my daughter so frequently has told me, am indeed the stereotypical mark ready for picking. If the dreaded "something" happens, who will know where I am and what has happened to me? After all, everyone is at home getting ready to celebrate the New Year.

The man doesn't talk. Once we are properly inside the tunnel, he gets ahead of me and I have to take three squishy steps to match each one of his powerfully steady stomps, and then, lo and behold, there are the steps going up. The man again walks behind me. I try hard not to imagine those strong huge hands closing around my throat, but the visualization is so strong that I have to turn around and look. His hands are hanging limp at his sides. He is looking down on his toes, clearly engaged in some thoughts of his own, far removed from both my throat and me. In spite of my down-filled coat, I am ice-cold and start to sneeze violently. Liquid pours out of my nostrils. There is no hankie in my pocket and I use the old sleeve method. The coat will have to go to the cleaners.

Unexpectedly, there is the light at the real end of the tunnel. This is no metaphor. This is a real light at the end of a real tunnel. The man and I both step out into the clear and cold Pennsylvania New-Year's-Eve sunlight, and there, right there, I kid you not, are the Penn Medicine buildings, just like I remembered them. So there, I am not insane after all. The man continues briskly to the right, and suddenly he looks like a friendly giant plodding awkwardly through the piled-up snow, while I must cross the street.

"Thank you!" I shout at him. "You get the guardian angel prize for 2013!"

"What do you know," he calls back. "That's what I always wanted! Happy New Year!" He waves me off.

"Happy New Year!" I wave back.

I arrive at the doctor's office exactly on time. I wait 30 minutes in the pleasantly decorated waiting room. I don't mind one bit. Time is what I have. I am evidently her last patient of 2013, and the wonderful Dr. Fleischman declares me splendidly healthy and tells me to keep on doing whatever it is that I am doing. Evidently I am doing it right.

I make my way back to the railroad station without incident or external assistance, happy in the sensation that Dr. Carol Rose Fleischman has just offered me the promise of another year of life. The train comes on time and takes me back to the wonders of the 30th Street Station. I linger a bit over the *New York Times* and the *Philadelphia Inquirer*. The pretzel booth offers great coffee. Both newspapers complain about the inadequate schools and the dysfunctional congress. As an official retiree, I need not fret about either. I am pretty much out of that game. Tomorrow there will be plenty of time to make resolutions and see if I can figure out ways to live up to my greatest and best potential. But right now let me be. Give me a break. Happy New Year!

BECOMING A DOCENT

"You need to do something serious and meaningful," my insightful daughter tells me, "and you won't be happy unless you are learning something."

She is right, of course. I had worked full-time over most of my life in situations that demanded constant intellectual growth, and here, suddenly, I am a retired lady of leisure. I am no more decrepit than I have been the previous year, when I still carried a full schedule of classes. Was it really just a few months ago, I had been considered a well-functioning member of the earning and the productive societies? Why had I so suddenly dropped everything, so willingly fled away from all of it to a new and unpredictable, and possibly meaningless life?

I had no answer. Honestly, I had never given life in retirement any thought. But now suddenly there was the intense need to be close to my daughters; to mourn together with them, to watch, within them, the genetic material so neatly deposited by my absent husband. Strangely, I found myself jealous of those genetic deposits in my daughters' faces, bodies, and movements—all so like those of my lost husband. I had been his closest person, as he had been mine; but they, not I, carried his genes and somehow, and with total illogic, I was envious.

I could and should have waited, of course. All the widows' advice books tell us not to change anything. "Wait a year before making any crucial decisions," is the repeated truism in these wise texts of guidance, but my widowhood had been sprung on me so suddenly, and I had not read the advice books for widows, and even if I had done so, I probably, in my frazzled state of mind, would not have paid any attention to them.

So, here I was, totally demoted from busy and engaged Dr. Hess, embraced by Arizona sunshine, to a wobbly, stranger to herself, pushing her shopping cart on the uneven sidewalks of rainy West Philadelphia, wondering where and how on earth I would find a foothold in my fractured new world.

"You must find something meaningful, mom," all three supportive daughters insist. I agree, of course, but I wonder what that meaningful thing is to be. Should I volunteer as a school tutor? Should I offer to peel potatoes in a soup kitchen? Should I help to slice cheese in the neighborhood coop? Should I dust the books in a public library? None of the above strikes me as particularly appealing or consequential. And I continue to wallow around in misery, boredom, and frustration. But, just as am about to sink into total funk, the answer comes blowing in with the wind, a wind peppered by Philadelphia drizzle.

The National Museum of American Jewish History is opening its doors at 5th and Market Streets, and is advertising for volunteer docents. Surely this is the place for me. I have, after all, functioned as a teacher of some sort for over 40 years, and I am a history buff. I have a Ph.D. under my belt as well as a 26-page resume that includes publications and teaching awards. Surely, they will welcome me with open arms.

"They're going to love you, mom," my daughters insist, and I believe them. Full of excitement I wander over to offer my services. The reception is distinctly chilly. Actually, they already have 250 volunteers lined up. Perhaps I would be interested in being a coat-checker, or a ticket collector? There might still be some room on those lists. I try to smile and note that, "I will think about it."

"Well, don't think too long because those volunteer lists are also filling up, and fast, too. And yes, we have very qualified folks in line —several retired physicians, quite a few former college instructors, many excellent retired classroom teachers, some lawyers and even a retired judge."

Much humbled, I leave with my resume tucked away. My endlessly supportive Philadelphia daughter is incensed. "That's ridiculous, mom! Who did you talk to? I can't believe that they won't take you! You are the perfect fit! I am going to make some phone calls," and she does.

I don't know whom she talks to, but two days later I get a phone call. I am on the list—evidently number 251, and they only need forty docents, but at least I am on the list. My heart sings! I send in my resume. I become a member of the museum, and follow several docent-led tours. I learn that American Jewish history begins in 1654 when 23 Jews arrive in New Amsterdam, and are almost kicked out by Peter Stuyvesant, who, I discovered, was a most unpleasant fellow. He surely didn't like Jews, but to give him credit, he didn't like many other people either. Is this, perhaps, why they sent him out to the colonies? I learn how the Jews, as peddlers, sold everything from pins to pianos on their journey from rug sack, to pushcart, to Jewish store and finally to ownership of Macy's department store. I learn about their contributions to the revolutionary and the civil wars. It is a spectacular journey of 350 years, a vibrant display of a people who worked hard to acculturate and yet managed to continue practicing and cherishing their own unique heritage.

I am in awe of the knowledgeable docents who tell me all this. I feel like Alice in Wonderland, and I don't want to leave. In the artifacts on display I find visual representation of the human soul. The very physical shape of the museum in its resemblance to an ocean liner inspires me with hope. I had, after all been an immigrant several times in my life. Could I immigrate and reintegrate once again on this ship of hope that gave such graphic and vivid legitimization of my experiences?

Weeks go by, and I know that my daughter has made several additional phone calls. I hear nothing. My ever-persistent daughter attempts to contact a cousin in Chicago, who seems to know someone influential. Nothing.

One day there is a telephone message. They want me to re-send my resume. Another three weeks go by. Then, just as I begin to think that maybe the soup kitchen will do, there is another message. I am invited for an interview. I have been through many interviews in my life, but I cannot remember a single invitation that brought about such a singular sense of anticipation and trepidation. I go clothes shopping at Macy's and Boyd's, and finally settle on an outfit from Loft—nice slacks and a femininely laced, yet professionally expressive blouse. I have my hair cut in a beauty parlor style (I usually cut my own), and I think seriously about hair color, but decide against it. I spend the nights prior to the appointment madly reading American History books. I don't feel American enough. After all, I did not go to elementary school in America.

A lovely young lady interviews me. She must be the age of my daughter. She encourages me to ask questions, and when I do, I notice that she is just about as nervous as I am. I wonder if this is a new job for her, and I feel strong vibes of sympathy between us. We part on what seem most cordial terms. A week later, I finally get the message. I have made it! I will participate in a year-long docent course that is about to begin.

My soul sings. I walk to the museum to pick up various forms that need to be signed. The secretaries are friendly. I am now part of the gang. And I so much need to be part of something. I express my appreciation and my hope to work with everyone.

"Well," she says, "We did have many good candidates, but we figured that anyone who has a daughter, pesky or not, a daughter who is willing to say so many good things about her mother over and over again, well, that mother probably deserves our closer attention."

MEETING CHARLES

"It's time you stop moping around," my friend Cindy says. "Honestly, you are an attractive woman, and we live in the new digital age. It's not all that hard to find a suitable man. Seriously, have you thought about online dating? Yes, I know. Don't tell me. There are ten eligible women for each desirable man. So what! Those 'desirables' get lonely like the rest of us! So, go for it, girl. What have you got to lose?"

What indeed?

I decide to do it!

The first thing is to find the picture that must be presented. It must be truthful but, of course, also as attractive as possible. Next, there is the writing of the bio–candid, yet intriguing. The real me, briefly encapsulated in its best possibilities. There is a rigid word limit, and that's a good thing. Otherwise, I might easily meander into a *David Copperfield* dissertation. Choices must be made. I have to create not only an attractive version of myself, but also one that will not disappoint when that magical first meeting occurs. Who do I want to be as I encapsulate my loneliness?

I get advice from many directions:

"Don't mention your Ph.D."

"Don't talk about being a Holocaust survivor. Such things might put off and intimidate men in your particular age-group."

"Please be real, but perhaps not, all that realistically real!"

"Men are romantic you know. Also, they scare easily!"

Eventually, I put things together and enter the fray.

After a trial week of "no response" two "winks" appear. A wink is the first sign of interest, and Cindy warns to take my time. "First chat a bit in writing, then move on to the telephone, and if you still like him, then set a date for coffee or perhaps lunch."

Her voice of experience makes sense, but I am too curious. I read the bios of my two winkers carefully, and I study their pictures. They both look like pleasant enough people, and I am suddenly so glad that this is not a beauty contest. Number one is called Morty, and he sends me both phone and e-mail contact. I reciprocate. He leaves several phone messages, but somehow, I can never find him in person. Number two is more cooperative. His bio he tells me that he too is a Holocaust child survivor, who spent the war years on false papers in Paris. He is a former electrical engineer. Well, perhaps this is a possibility. Who knows? He says that he loves romantic walks on beaches. Boy, this fellow knows how to charm a woman. I give him credit for that.

I suggest that we meet for coffee, and when he asks where, I, without too much thought, propose the 30th Street Railroad Station in Central Philly. It happens to be one of the few places I know in Philadelphia, and he agrees. I have no idea that he, later, will give me enormous credit for the choice.

"Wow!" he, much later, tells me. "I loved that woman already! She must be very smart. That railroad station is probably the safest place to meet in Philadelphia. After all, it has its own police department, and if she doesn't like me, she can always just walk away."

A railroad station is a fluid place, where people come and go, and where you truly can have just a cup of coffee. No menu. No embarrassing waiter waiting time. No effort needed to swallow food one doesn't like, no need to get up and leave the table as waiters politely offer you "anything else?"

So, we meet. The talk flows easily, and I am surprised when my watch registers two hours. *Mensch* seems to be written all over him. What is a mensch, you might ask. Well, if you are Jewish, you probably already know, but perhaps you're not. Don't worry about it. "Nobody is perfect," as a well-known Jewish comedian once noted. Mensch implies decency, commitment, and integrity, also a sense of seriousness mingled with dry humor and an appreciation of life. I liked the sense of menschness that I right away detect in this fellow. Toward the end of that first meeting, he is holding my hand, and I very much like that. We agree to meet again.

It has been some years now, and it seems to work. In many ways, he is the complete opposite of John. John towered above me by at least five inches. Charles and I are about the same height. John was never seriously interested in food. He ate when he was hungry. Charles is a gourmet. After all, he grew up in France. And like me, he is a Holocaust survivor. To me, noting these similarities and differences, shows that you can love many different kinds of people. Ever so slowly, our relationship offers both perks and plateaus. One thing is certain. We worry much less about small stuff. We are grateful for a deep friendship and a warm, physical closeness. We are both grateful about things that at a younger age we might have taken for granted.

For some time I don't really know how to define this new relationship. I lack the proper terminology. As I write this, I have known him for about three years, and, in many ways, we have grown close. Although, to tell the truth, sometimes I feel that we are still pretty much in "best behavior" mode.

And what's wrong with that? I, rather petulantly, ask myself. Perhaps I feel that this is not genuine behavior. Not the way real people deal with real feelings. On the other hand, in one's 80s, one does become a different kind of person. One realizes that one's time is limited, and really not to be wasted on "small stuff," not to be fretted away on petty arguments or concerns. Time, at this interesting stage in life, has to be held and culled and treasured and this is done better with a partner, and it is a privilege to have one. No mistake on that.

Like me, Charles spent some years after the war in Europe, like me he is a widower who experienced a lifetime within the embrace, comfort, and devotion of a long and happy marriage. Like me, he was lonely and longing for intimacy and the kind of support that one finds in loving affiliations.

When trying to introduce him to friends, I find no proper term in English to define us. In Swedish, there is rich taxonomy. Someone who is not your legally married spouse but with whom you now share living space is known as your *sahmboo* (literally translated as "my live-together with"). If you take turns living occasionally in his and occasionally in her household, the official term becomes my *turboo* (my-taking-turns with). If he has more or less become your steady significant, but you have chosen to remain living separately, he is your *sehrboo* (my live-separately-with). Adult offsprings who choose to return home to live with their parents are known as *mamaboo*. By now, you have, no doubt figured out that the word "boo", spelled "B-O" in Swedish, means "live" in the sense of "dwell" or "reside." In English, however, we still cling to decayed social forms, refusing to make the linguistic jump through the hoops of our new societal assignments.

When we meet, he is 84 to my 78, and we seem to have grown into a newly-minted couple of sorts. It seems a bit far-fetched to call him my boyfriend. After all, even if it doesn't feel that way, it has certainly been a long time since anyone has called him a boy. Referring to him as, just "my friend" seems too vague and unsatisfactory. My "significant other," is too technical, too academic.

"This is my friend," I say in a rather non-committal way. Let them make of it what they will. We seem to go together well.

People smile at us as we walk on Philadelphia sidewalks holding hands. Such newly acquired social approval warms us in its smugness. We seem to fold easily into each other's thinking patterns.

"Are you two a number?" one direct individual asks.

"Yes," I nod. We are indeed a number. So, should I be introducing him as "my number?" Perhaps my new number? My recent number? My most recent number?

We do comfort one another. He opens doors for me. He is, after all, a gentleman of the 50s. I sense his jealousy as I talk to other men. Somehow these masculine idiosyncrasies warm my shrinking soul. I see laughter and pleasure in his eyes after a hug. We are a good cure for mutual aloneness. Shared sadness mutes grief, and allows a sense of new identity to have clearer focus. Love seems to wrap us with a sense of dignity.

There is, of course the sharing of our histories. We never knew the people we used to be when we were young, when we were parents of young children, when we were struggling professionals, when we were middle-aged.

So, now we meet one another as grandparents and parents of adult children and of grandchildren that we don't share. Still, we, who cherished our marriages, both sense that it is ever so much easier to experience old age as a couple.

Old age poses its own definitions, its own reasons, its own demands, and needs, and survival strategies. These we can share. We provide forgotten facts and words for each other, as the senior-moments hit at diverse times and in surprising locations. We are at an interesting stage. Experiences are considered more carefully. The small stuff is easier to recognize and discard. The moment is more clearly recorded for its nuances and its melodies.

We don't like to eat the same things. I favor Chinese and Indian. He loves French and Japanese, but fortunately, we both like fish. He is much more of a gourmet than I am. I have a sweet tooth. He doesn't. He introduces me to wines. Are these things important? I don't know. Sometimes I am even surprised when the differences emerge.

A lot comes with survivor osmosis. When he tells me that for years after the war, he was terrified of people in uniforms, it sparks a memory. I vividly remember these fears, and I am surprised that I had actually managed to forget them. When a fire truck zooms by with its particular sound of warning, both of us recall the sirens that moved us to shelters. Both of us carry the survivor load of sadness and gratitude. He finds meaning by being a witness. He is an excellent speaker, and his survivor stories are high drama. He tells them well and feels strongly about the need to bear witness.

"There are so few of us left," he says. "Soon there will no one, and then people will start believing that it never happened. If only one person among those in the audiences who hear me takes my story to the world and negates the 'It never-happened functionaries,' then I will have done my job!"

He, indeed, does his job passionately, with dignity and style. He takes it to schools, conferences, and community centers. He always shows up when called, and his reputation has soared. He is the rock star on the Holocaust-survivor circuit. I, on the other hand, still find speaking out painful, even thinking about it is painful for me, but I do appreciate what he is doing and I feel proud of him. And then, very gradually, I, too, inspired by him, start speaking out.

Often when we walk together, I feel a certain softness encasing us. We live in the here-and-now. Here and now is who we are. Here and now is what we have. It's a homecoming of sorts—our lucky numbers!

THE GOOD CITIZEN

The USA votes for its 44th president in November of 2012. The incumbent, President Barak Obama, is the candidate of the Democratic Party. His opponent, Mitt Romney, is on the Republican ticket. It seems to be a very close election and every vote counts. I am determined that mine should be included in the final count. The question is whether the state of Pennsylvania, in which I now reside, will allow me to exercise this obligation of good citizenship.

I moved to Philadelphia in the fall of 2011 right before primary elections in which I definitely wanted to participate. After all, as a newly minted docent at The National Museum of American Jewish History, I had just recently learned that in the year of 1790, no less a personage than George Washington himself had, as a result of his visit to the Jewish congregation of Newport, Rhode Island, granted "the stock of Abraham" free and full citizenship provided they "demean themselves as good citizens." And, indeed, as such a "good citizen," I have never yet missed voting in any election.

The first time I voted on a national scale was for John F.

Kennedy in 1961. The memorable aspect of that polling experience was seeing so many nuns in the beautiful, medieval habits, which they at that time were still wearing, lined up to make their presence felt. At the time, I had secretly wondered whether this might just have been the first time these ladies had shown up in such great numbers to demonstrate their duty of citizenship.

As a new Pennsylvanian in this year of 2012, I am anxious to prove my own legitimacy, and I battle the subways and buses from West Philly to find my way to the proper office, where I produce my valid Arizona driver's license together with bills addressed to my present Philadelphia address, and I receive a temporary voter ID, and am told that the permanent one will be arriving in the mail, which indeed it does a week later.

In the primary election, I find my way to my assigned polling place, where I am delighted to discover that my name already appears on the official lists, and where the nice volunteer ladies welcome me with, "We have been waiting for you!"

I proudly cast my primary selection, receiving a sticker of recognition. It says: "I Voted."

As the presidential election approaches, however, new situations bring on new demands. A recent law in Pennsylvania proclaims that every voter is required to produce an "acceptable photo identification" before being allowed to cast the ballot. The ID must be Pennsylvania minted. Thus, my Arizona driver's license will no longer do. There are evidently two possibilities in a case such as mine, and I hear these options articulated daily on my local radio station:

1. I could possibly exchange my Arizona driver's license for a Pennsylvania one.
2. I could just obtain a voter I.D. card that would feature my likeness. All I have to do is report to my local Penn DOT office, and I will be served.

Eager to comply, I once more make my way from West Philly to 8th and Arch in Center City for my first visit to the establishment.

Penn DOT is an enormous room, densely populated in what appears to be over one hundred compactly seated, impatient, and depressed souls. My ticket number is 840. There is no seat available, and I join a line of standers in the back of the room. This gives me some time to study the crowd. It consists mostly of the young and heavily tattooed. There is a low murmur of conversation, and occasionally I pick up a snippet. I hear things like, "I could really kill him for that." Intently I listen for the crux of what could be an interesting story, but the rest is just a jumble of sound. Often, I seem to hear, the phrase, "And I was sayin'..." without ever being able to actually become aware of what on earth it was that the speaker was, indeed, saying. "You know" and "like" appear to still be constant staples of conversational English, other than that, I hear nothing of great interest. Maybe my sense of hearing is going. But then, quite suddenly there is some diverting noise. Up front by the number-givers, an elderly woman on crutches is throwing a fit.

"I am calling Harrisburg," she screams. "I am not coming down here again. I called and this is the information I was given. What do you people think that you are doing?"

This outburst is followed by muffled noises, as well as by bored but sympathetic nods from the surrounding crowd.

"They're sure doing a lot to keep folks from voting," the angry young man next to me declares.

"You can say that again," his female companion agrees.

"Bastards!" says the young man, following it with a mumbled phrase, which my sense of hearing cannot untangle.

Seven counters call out numbers, but mine is still far down the line. My new-fangled cell phone, with which I am still doing battle, tells me that one hour has passed. I am still standing in the back of the room, but now in the front row two seats are being vacated and I decide to take my chances for yet another half hour. This time, I

219

find myself in front of two young ladies—one is complaining bitterly about a lost love, while the second one seems to offer consolation.

"So, like he says to me, like you take the TV. Can you, like, believe that? That's what I get out of, like, the relationship," the wounded one complains.

"Hey, you are so lucky that the bastard, like, walked out," the consoling one proposes.

I wish that I had brought a book. Again, I do my best to pick up bits of possibly interesting conversation. Behind me a woman provides her companion a snippet.

"So, we were nine of us, and only one bathroom," she moans. "Can you believe that? And now we are five and there are three bathrooms, and someone always has to pee. Can you beat that?"

"Uh-huh," her companion acknowledges. The rest is a blur of sound, in the midst of announcements from the loud speakers.

Half an hour later, I decide to leave, which I really have to do in order not to miss the next lecture at OLLI. I grant my 840 number to the grateful 960 guy. And that concludes my first visit to the Penn DOT center. At any rate, by listening to the conversations around me, I realize that I might not have brought all the required documents.

A week later, I try again. This time I am armed with my valid American passport, and two letters that prove that I indeed presently reside on S. 47th street in Philadelphia, Pennsylvania, as well as the required check for $29.50 Unfortunately, I arrive on a Monday, when the office is open, but does not deal with ID questions.

"Do come back tomorrow," I am advised. And that is my second try at a visit with PennDOT.

Persistent as I am in asserting my rights of citizenship, I do show up on Tuesday at 11:30 a.m., again armed with the required documents. This time, I have also brought my old friend, *David Copperfield*. By 1:00 p.m. I have reached chapter 4, and gotten

David as far as "Salem House School," when my number 436 is actually called, and I gratefully approach counter seven.

"Yes, I do have a valid American passport. Yes, I do have two official letters that proclaim my present address. Yes, I do have an Arizona driver's license."

And the kind clerk checks these items off her official list. But, bless it, will there always be that crucial "But?" Here it comes: "You also need to bring your Social Security Card. No, your Medicare Card won't do. Oh, you think that you might have lost your Social Security card. That card that you so proudly obtained at age sixteen, 60 years ago? Well, lucky you! It's really easy to get a new one. The office is just three blocks away. But, of course, they do close at 1:00 p.m. You might want to try tomorrow." And that ends my third visit to Penn DOT.

On Wednesday at 11:00 a.m., I sit at the "Social Security Office" on 15th and Market. At 12:30 p.m. I receive a letter, which states my social security card will shortly be mailed to me. A week later, I indeed receive it, and ready myself for another journey to Penn DOT, where I arrive at 11:00 o'clock armed with my valid Arizona driver's license, my valid American passport, the two letters, which affirm my Philadelphia residency, the crucial check, and, of course, my newly minted social security card. I have also brought along *David Copperfield*, whom I just pick up as he is about to marry beloved little Dora. My number is 683, and it is called at counter four, just as I reach Dora's deathbed.

"Birth certificate?" the perky young clerk inquires.

"Sorry, I don't have one. I was born in Poland," I explain. "But I do have a valid US passport."

"I will need your naturalization papers."

"But they are in a different name."

She will have to ask about that.

"Was there an official name change? A marriage certificate?" she consults again.

It seems that the valid American passport will do, after all. I

221

breathe again. All my other papers are in order. I can't believe it. I am actually going to get a brand new Pennsylvania driver's license. I will become a real registered person with a genuine photo I.D.

My cup runneth over! I beam with friendly feeling towards one and all. The perky clerk actually smiles back! And I am sent off to take the eye test, which surely will be no problem for me. Hey, I just recently passed one in Arizona.

Fearlessly, I face the machine, and much to my horror discover that I cannot read a single word in line four. I read lines one, two, and three just fine—but—and here is that "BUT" again, line four has to be read. They give me a form for the eye-doctor.

I stand there begging. "Couldn't I, at least, get a photo I.D. just to show at a polling place? A photo I.D. that has nothing to do with driving—an identity card of sorts?"

"No, that would not be allowed."

"And why not?"

"Well, two I.D. cards from different states are not legally allowed."

"And why not?"

"Well, you could possibly vote here, then hop on a plane to Arizona, and vote there as well. That's the voter fraud that we are trying to eliminate, after all."

Much dejected I leave Penn DOT, ending my fourth visit there.

I tell my story to several new friends.

"Just lie!" I am advised. "Don't tell them that you have an Arizona Driver's license. Just ask for a voter I.D. card."

I follow their advice. Once more on a bright Tuesday morning, I am given number 206 and prepare myself with a lengthy and careful reading of *The New York Times*.

When my turn comes, I gingerly approach counter eight, and present my documents to an elderly male clerk. He looks me straight in the eye and asks the fatal question, "Do you have a valid driver's license in any other state?"

And then, to my horror and chagrin, I discover that I cannot tell a lie. I cannot lie to this official. Not even to get to vote. The memory of President Clinton, who almost was impeached because he lied to the FBI, flashes through my mind. *Never lie to the FBI*, I tell myself and firmly reject the notion that this particular official may not fit that picture. I swallow hard, tell the truth, and give up my quest for a Pennsylvania voter photo I.D. Yes, I know, don't tell me. I can get to vote merely by showing my valid American passport together with two letters addressed to my present abode, and I will, of course use that privilege. But I did so want that nifty little card that would fit snugly into my wallet, and proclaim my existence, and suppose, just suppose that I were not a frequent traveler with an updated and valid passport? How many people are there in that particular situation? Or, suppose, I could not afford that check of $29.50 now required? Also, assume that I did not have the strength to make those repeated visits to Penn.DOT? I recall the angry lady on crutches. There must be many of those. Did she ever make the call to Harrisburg? Was she able to talk with a real person there, or was she forced into the finger-exercise of unresponsive button pushing?

"Bastards!" said the young man "Bastards!"

Yes, at this moment, frankly, I can't think of a better way of phrasing it.

MEMORY OF FORGETTING

I am on the roof of our 30-story apartment house. This summer of 2016, our roof has been turned into a city-garden utopia. Blooming shrubs in colorful containers are on display everywhere, especially for this "Sips" event that we celebrate every Thursday evening and to which we bring our own beverage and a snack to share. The atmosphere is lively. Lots of chitchat about this and that, restaurants, movies worth seeing, the weather, all interesting and relevant topics, but not in any sense controversial. Most of us are women, after all, and at this sensitive stage in life, so many more of the feminine gender seem to have stayed around. This topic in itself might become worthy of consideration, but solely in "female only" groupings. Since here and there on our roof garden we also sport occasional folk of the male persuasion, we don't want to enter provocative territory.

Over the years, we have all learned about the great sensitivity of the "fragile male ego," so we step lightly and speak with care. With such care in mind and on tongue, I also notice that even though a certain topic is, at this point in time on everyone's mind no one dares to mention the complex issue of our very acrimonious presidential election, which surely intrigues all of us but if brought into a conversational circle, at this time, could well create the kind of problematic atmosphere which one definitely is trying to avoid here on a peaceful and flowering summer evening.

On a personal level, I am working on trying to remember people's names, a skill which seems to grow weaker each day. At this particular point in time, for example, I have just been introduced to Bernadette and her friend Irene.

The name Bernadette is a cinch. There are many stories connected to it, and stories are my forte. Does this Bernadette know the story of St. Bernadette of Lourdes? That wonderful miracle tale told so well by Franz Werfel, the German Jew, who fled to Los Angeles during the Holocaust? If she doesn't know the story, why, I am most eager to tell her, but I needn't. Her mother had loved the name. Had loved it so much that she decided to give it to her daughter, and my new friend, whose name I will certainly always remember, tells me that she too loves her own name. She knows the whole story of St. Bernadette. Although she has never heard of Franz Werfel, she had seen the movie.

Me? I am happy! I will never forget this new neighbor's name. But, how on earth and why had I remembered the name of Franz Werfel, about whom I certainly had not thought at all for at least 40 years?

As I relax and sit back in my glowing Bernadettian pleasure, there suddenly appears to be an unforeseen problem: That other lady sitting right next to Bernadette, that lady to whom I had just been, so recently, introduced. What was her name again? Susan? Stella? Cathleen? For the life of me I can't remember. The name just won't come to me, no matter how hard I try to focus. This is embarrassing. Should I make a fool of myself and ask her? But she had just told me. Just screw up your courage and tell the lovely woman that in your Bernadettian excitement, you have forgotten her name, and then, for heaven's sake, try not to forget it again right away.

And then the nice lady turns to me with a beautiful smile, "I so much enjoyed hearing everything that you had to tell Bernadette," she says, "that I forgot your name, and I, by the way, I am Irene, just in case you forgot."

I do love that Irene. I'll never forget her, but I might forget her name. The forgetfulness is a dreadful thing. But it seems to hit all of us who have reached a certain number. And there is comfort in numbers, and I love to be around others of the same number.

Here on the roof, I recall other times and places when our numbers were clearly in evidence. One day in class at OLLI, where those of a certain age partake in the feeding of our souls, a gentleman in front of me raised his hand to ask a pertinent question. When the instructor called on him, he suddenly looked blank and admitted to having forgotten his question. One might at such a time have felt a certain derision or even ridicule from members of the class, and such disdain would probably have emerged in a younger group, but here among our numbers, a deep sense of commonality and team spirit ensued. Smiles of understanding, cohesion and camaraderie pervaded. Everywhere people were smiling and nodding their heads in a spirit of harmony.

"Yup, that happens to me all the time," appeared to be a generally accepted class theme song.

The other day my friend, Charles, and I stood at my window examining the new apartment house that had just been completed.

"We really need a pair of mmmm..."

"Yes," I agreed. "We do need a pair of mmmm..."

We look at each other in despair. Both of us make the shape of a pair of binoculars with our hands. But the word "binocular" has completely escaped both of us.

I remember it in Swedish. It's a *kikare*.

I also remember it in Hebrew. It's a *mishkefet*.

He remembers it in French. The French logically see it in the plural. In French it is *jumelles*.

So, we look it up in the French/ English dictionary, and there it

226

is bold as brass—binoculars. Wow! How could we have forgotten that? And in English it is sort of plural as well. Now what would you say, "Where are the binoculars?" or "Where is the binoculars?" Or perhaps, "Where is the binocular?" No, that doesn't sound right. The "*bi*" there, at the beginning of the word, indicates a couple, so that would automatically make the word plural. Would it really now? A "bicycle" has climbed into the singular world in English, even though it probably started out with a two-wheeled notion. Well, for the time being, there are the binoculars in glorious plurality ensconced in our challenged minds, for as long as they last, lest we forget!

THE QUESTION THEY WILL
INVARIABLY ASK

It is Thanksgiving Day 2017, the quintessentially American holiday that everyone can love. We all have something to be grateful for, and everyone's God is present to receive the message. Even the God of unbelievers finds him or herself, perhaps a bit annoyed, but, nevertheless present.

I have been invited to a huge family affair, but for some reason my hosts have chosen an evening rather than a mid-day meal, which places me in the position of having to spend a long day in a state of temporary alienation. So, I have time, wanted or unwanted, for unplanned contemplation; frankly, a state of mind which I mostly attempt to avoid.

I am downstairs at Nelson's Grocery store, which also serves as a place to have coffee. I go there often. The clerks know me, greet me, and offer me a sense of fellowship, tenuous though it might be. Coffee and chocolate are prizes with which I reward myself for having made my bed, gotten dressed, and dutifully swallowed my morning medications.

My contemplation this morning takes me to the unwanted question that so often is placed before me, as I conduct younger visitors through the museum of American Jewish History. The museum, being the story of the American adventure, does not feature the Holocaust as one of its central exhibitions. The topic is actually restricted to one dark corridor. Nevertheless, the Holocaust is a subject recently introduced to the Pennsylvania school curriculum, and thus, it becomes central in the minds of my young visitors, who quite frequently come to the museum as part of their studies.

"Why didn't God do anything?" they ask.

"Where was God when all this was happening?"

And the ubiquitous one from the adult accompanying them, "Can you still believe in God after all this?" And then the often repeated, "Clearly, there is no God, if he allowed such things to happen."

Such questions and comments are, of course, quite understandable. The perpetrators who built and operated the highly efficient industrial death complexes were not incompetent, or primitive losers. They were efficient functionaries, competent professionals, skilled engineers, and knowledgeable academics. They came from a long, well-oiled, and sophisticated culture that had earned worldwide fame and had a sterling reputation. Yet here they were not only building factories for efficient murder, but also managing these industries, approving of the institutions, and being mostly supporting of and participating in the continued functions of the well-functioning mass-murder of innocent men, women and children. How could such a thing be? How could such an aberration have happened and where oh where was God?

Where is the benevolent God?

Where is the divine plan?

Where is that one and only, whose name we cannot mention?

Where is the divine who never sleeps? The guardian of Israel?

Who is he? Is he?

Where is he?

Why is he?

And how can I still find him?

I who, at age five, lost my parents to the furnaces of Treblinka?

My God is there because I want God to be there. My God idea is still what has gotten me up in the morning. This morning, to be exact. I carry on because of that mystical, unexplainable essence of redemption. Yes, it is as simple as all that.

One thing my God is not: a puppeteer. He doesn't pull the strings of his creation. We dance on our own. We have been given minds, but we must learn how to use those all on their own. And yes, there is an instruction book, but, like these things go, it has to be read, understood, and practiced.

Humanity of my understanding is programmed for goodness in a long course of graduate studies. Some of us are further along than others. Some of us are vegetarians, others still have a long way to go in that one little course diversion. Some have dedicated their lives to the service of selfless good. Some are still in the cage of self-satisfaction.

The course demands serious graduate work, while some of us are still in nursery school, but we too will get there. The grading curve is rather steep. I and most of my friends get about a C minus. How long will it take to pass into redemption? Six million of my tribe died. Each one with his/her own death; each with a penny's worth of redemption.

I lost my parents when I was five. I remember walking between them, one of my hands on each side holding on with a blessed sense of belonging. Was this a half penny for redemption? It was delicious. Someday, humanity will have earned a Ph.D., and God will be there for the graduation ceremony—perhaps for the beginning of a post-graduate course. The process of creation is constant and everlasting. God is there. He just doesn't pull any strings. Creation is a self-guided project—perhaps with some committee work. Agony, humiliation, and destruction of human dignity can never serve as justice.

Here is something that I once overheard in Ravensbrück:

"When the war is over, they will parade Hitler in a cage on top of a truck, and we will all be given knives, so that each one of us can cut a piece of his flesh. We will then sprinkle salt on each wound, and listen with joy to his screams."

I was then a very childish nine-year-old, but I shut my mind on that sense of misplaced justice. We are all enrolled in the University of Human Perfection. We are endlessly creating God. Who is God? Where is he? He is us –you and me. We are the creators. We are also the creation. Here we are, here we were, and here we will be.

FOR TEACHERS AND THEIR STUDENTS

Maybe this chapter is just for teachers. Or maybe it is for everyone who has ever loved or ever hated a teacher. And that seems to be just about everyone.

It isn't easy to capture the classroom—that nebulous, ephemeral, messy place that can appear so neat and proper with its rows of desks and that eternal board—black no longer, chalk gone, markers running dry, but never mind. It is still the place where dreams start, where hearts are broken and mended, where self-image is built or destroyed, where notions become possibilities and possibilities spring into action.

Is there a place to hide in the back row? In the classroom, one can find spaces of belonging or slink into spaces of exclusion. How is it that ideas flourish in such dull territory? How can the geography be so different when seen from the one desk up front, the "teacher's desk," facing the multitude of rows, and a seat in one of those rows? How can this innocuous and lackluster territory become a place of pride as well as a place of both eviction and inclusion?

I was a classroom teacher for 48 years. I tried to do the job well but how does doing well in teaching look? The better it is done, the easier it looks. In my teacher prep classes I have often asked my students to describe their favorite teacher. What made that teacher so unique? There does seem to be one teacher like that for just about everyone, and certainly for those who intend to enter the profession. The answers are invariably the same. It basically boils down to "How that teacher made me feel." Seldom, in my experience, is there talk about intelligence, clarity, or even humor. Seldom has there been talk of scholarship or organization—those textbook requirements of the profession.

I had always wanted my classroom to be a place where students felt safe to grow, a place where ideas were valued for their own sake and not just for future benefit. I wanted a sense of respect, a sense of excitement, a sense of hope. Did I accomplish some of that? Perhaps I will never know. Most of the time, I was worried about the flow of my lesson plans, the disruptive students, the organization of the blackboard, the visit of the principal, the progress of the test scores, the marking of papers—ah, yes that endless ceaseless marking of papers. When teaching, one climbs a glass mountain, and one slips, one gets up and keeps on climbing. The important thing is never to stop, never to get stuck holding on to the fear of it.

I got my first teaching job in Port Washington, New York, in 1957 when I was 21 years old. My students were kids in their early and late teens. I wore spike-heeled shoes and nylon stockings to distinguish my grown-up teacher-self from that of the students whose outfits included the required oxfords and bobby socks.

Each morning, I conscientiously checked the full-length mirror to see that the seams of my nylons were straight. It wasn't easy to get those seams straight. To indicate my adult status, I also wore a pearl necklace, and occasionally attached a cameo pin to my collar —anything to create a dignified teaching persona. Keep in mind that I was teaching Shakespeare to native-born American students, when I myself had spoken English for only five years. It was a big "fake it till you make it" thing, long before that particular maxim had been coined.

In the spring of 1957, I was hired by Dr. Hall, whose first name I no longer remember and maybe never even knew. He had arrived from New York at Indiana State Teachers' College in Terre Haute, Indiana to interview prospective teachers. Lucky for me, there was in the late 50s a great shortage of teachers in the USA, and from what I was told by the employment office at Indiana State Teachers' College (ISTC) it was because of this shortage that Dr. Hall was scouring the heartland. He was a Colorado man, who found himself as superintendent of schools in Port Washington, New York—a district rather heavily populated by Jews.

"He preferred teachers from the real American core," I was told. Having noted my high grades and the fact that the faculty had voted for me as "Miss Indiana State" that year, Dr. Hall decided to interview me. My personal goal was to get to New York to meet Jews, but in Dr. Hall's mind, I was evidently a pleasant Hoosier girl. He was a tall man in his prime, immaculately dressed in the required double-breasted blue suit accentuated by the red tie. An office on the third floor of the language-arts building had been set aside for the interviews. I climbed the stairs on legs of jelly. I was about to fulfil my dream of becoming an independent professional. I was about to finally fly on my own. This interview simply had to work. Dr. Hall was seated behind an imposing desk, and he rose to greet me, obviously trying to put me at ease.

"A pleasure to be talking with 'Miss Indiana State,'" he said. "I see that you have been preparing yourself to be a high school teacher of English and French. We do need teachers of English in Port Washington both in high school and in junior high school. Now tell me, young lady, which would you prefer high school or junior high school?"

Amazingly, yes, even now 54 years later, I still find it astonishing that I proceeded, without the slightest awareness of doing so, to follow a superb interview strategy. I only wish that I had remembered it during all the later interviews of my life. At that moment, I asked Dr. Hall a very relevant question, and I did so tactfully and reverently, acknowledging his superior understanding and awareness, but taking the focus entirely away from me and placing it on him.

"You have so much experience in these things," I earnestly said. "And honestly, I don't yet know anything. What exactly is the difference between teaching in high school and teaching in junior high school?"

Dr. Hall smiled warmly in benevolent condescension, and proceeded to talk for about half an hour about the developmental stages of the teen years, the variety of discipline issues, and the quality of educational structures. When he finished, I simply said, "Thank you. That was very informative. I think that I want to teach high school."

"You are hired," Dr. Hall said.

Later, in the fall of the year, when I arrived in Port Washington, New York, and started my work at Paul D. Schreiber High School, Jewish faculty members howled when I told my story. Dr. Hall was evidently known for his attempts to bring "real American teachers" into the system, and his inadvertent choice of me for the job struck everyone as a great joke.

"This is too much," chortled Lee Ashenbrener, who hired me to teach in the Reform Temple Sunday School. "The guy goes out there just to get away from all the Jews to find us the real McCoy, teachers from the heartland—real American teachers for our kids, and he brings you, for God's sake, a Jewish Holocaust survivor—that's rich. That's really rich."

That was the beginning of my close-to-50-year long teaching career. I did take off seven years when I had small children. And going back to teach in Israel, after that seven-year break, was traumatic, to say the least. The entire Israeli culture including, and perhaps especially the school culture, was very foreign to me. My Hebrew was still weak, and for a year or two, to put it mildly, I was a very inadequate teacher. I didn't know the rules. For example, I didn't know that students are allowed to leave if a teacher arrives more than ten minutes late for class.

One day, when I stopped on the stairway to speak with a parent, and thus arrived late, I discovered to my dismay, that my entire class except for two students had disappeared. I became angry, and made inappropriate remarks to the two good students who had waited for me. My behavior was completely out of line, and created an unpleasant atmosphere in the classroom until the end of the semester.

Later, when I became more experienced, I learned that in a case where a class disappears, I should have just calmly continued the lesson with the few students who were left, and the hooky-playing would, believe it or not, one by one traipse, rather shame-facedly, back into the room.

For several years afterward, I would run the other way when I encountered former students from those early years. But I did learn.

What exactly did I learn? I learned to print clearly on the board. I learned that issues of importance had to be repeated at least three times, but each time in a slightly different way. I learned that the best questions were the ones to which I did not have the answers. I learned that students can help one another better than I can help them; I learned that a whispered voice is a better attention getter than a shouted one. I learned that correction is a subtle and intricate business, and that one well-designed correction might bring results, while many, no matter how judicious, will doubtlessly bring about failure. Mostly, I learned that I had to use my own personality to build a teaching repertoire, and that the models, which I treasured from former teachers, had to be adjusted to fit my particular way of doing things.

By the time I retired in 2011, I had taught high school in New York and Massachusetts. I had taught high school in Israel for 24 years. I had taught teachers in Israel, in Taiwan, in Mexico, in

Turkey, in Great Britain, in Tucson, Arizona, and finally in Yuma, Arizona. I became somewhat of an ESL (English as a Second Language) expert, writing textbooks and teacher resource books on the topic.

Teaching is an emotionally loaded as well as intellectually engrossing profession. It fills you up in a way that can only be compared to an intensely burning love affair. You constantly think about it, dream about it, worry about it, revel in it and try to improve on it. You are never good enough for it. When you travel, you buy the poster that will work well into your Friday's lesson plan. When you meet new people, you notice those who might turn into good guest speakers in your classroom. When you read, the yellow highlighter is never far away to note what you should really have known and used last Tuesday. You constantly rearrange your units, elaborate or simplify your lesson plans, find new psychological evidence that the way you handled George or Susie, who graduated six years ago, was totally misguided. You gradually learn that in the classroom you are not the star. You are mostly a stage manager. In a successful learning environment, the learners are the stars. But certainly you also must occasionally take on leading actor roles. You must also write the script of the play, direct the performance, critique the show, read and ponder the student paper reviews, and re-write the script. And do it all over again for the next day's lessons. There is always the lesson you plan, the lesson you teach, and the lesson you wish that you had taught. The above are all well-known clichés, but clichés wouldn't have become clichés, if they were not true or certainly well researched and tested.

If you stay in the field for any length of time, the same old pendulum will, of course, strike you many times. By "pendulum" I mean, those heavily loaded theoretical dictums from above—the theorists, the textbook publishers, the departments of education the superintendents, often even the principals. Teachers live inside a vulnerable profession. Teacher-bashing has become an international sport. Teachers can, and often are, blamed for all the world's woes. Those who observe teachers frequently haven't the slightest idea of what they are looking at.

Your kid refuses to do his homework. Just blame the teacher. She (and, of course it will most likely be a "she") doesn't inspire, didn't clarify, and doesn't understand. Johnny scores poorly on a test, compared to Akihiko, his Japanese counterpart. Blame Johnny's teachers. They don't know their subject matter. They don't teach the important facts. They don't demand enough. They demand the wrong things. Let's fire the teachers and all will be well, until the next round anyway. Amazingly, the teachers mostly take it all in stride. They get lemons thrown at them and they promptly make lemon pie. They are bombarded by constantly fluctuating methodologies—direct instruction; student involvement; lots of projects; projects are busy work, the grammar-based method; the no-grammar-at-all method; the teach-to-the-test formula; the testing-is-outrageous formula. Whatever you say, boss. We are teachers. We have learned to swing on a wing, walk on a tight rope, and dance with the music. Teachers serve as social workers, parent-substitutes, psychologists, and police, and they must learn how to do all of it in their own personal style. Woe to the teacher who tries to imitate her own "great teacher." She will invariably fall on her face. She just isn't that teacher—no matter how wonderfully the memory projects itself.

When I worked with teachers, who were striving for the best methodology, I worked them to create a room where the teacher was a stage director rather than the chief actor.

I will always remember my visits to two superb 1st grade teachers, Maria Gutierrez and Theresa Gonzales. Maria was a fantastic organizer and she ran a tight ship. She took attendance in a jiffy; her stacks of paper were alphabetically arranged. Pictures, scissors, glue, and paper clips were all in place. Her billboards were set in a totally symmetrical display. She gave directions clearly and succinctly and multi-tasked with flare. I thought that she couldn't be topped, but then I went across the hall to observe Theresa. Theresa was just as organized but in a completely different way. Her bulletin boards were not quite as arranged, but students' work was on display—as put together by students. The boards were lovely; yet poles apart from the geometrical line-ups in Maria's class. There was a certain surrealism and impressionism involved. Theresa had no idea where the scissors, or the tape, or the attendance list were kept. But she had students assigned to each of these chores and they knew and kept track of everything, taking great pride in their responsibilities. Lists of who was responsible for what task were posted and adhered to and students were taking their jobs seriously.

"I just can't worry about these things," Theresa told me. Her classroom ran just as smoothly as Maria's. I found it more relaxed and student-friendly and every bit as functional. Both teachers had found their personal approach. They were both fabulous. But Picasso is not going to paint like Rembrandt, and should never try to. Teaching requires that certain aspects of classroom protocol are observed. For example, there must be a bulletin board. But where the bulletin board appears, how it looks and what its function is can vary according to the skills and interests of the teacher and the needs of the students.

Teaching is both art and craft. Craft can be observed, demonstrated, taught, practiced and learned. Art, on the other hand has to be there, and be recognized. It can never be overshadowed by craft. Craft is there to service art.

I worked hard on trying to be a good teacher. But when I look back on my 47-year-long career, the things that spring to mind, in spite of all the loving notes, the end-of-year flowers, and the accolades of praise, the strongest memories are mostly the dreadful things—the student in Quincy, Massachusetts who promised to kill me, the class in Israel that created a play based on jokes about me, or the cheaters who took me for a wimp and got away with it.

Teachers are people who constantly have nightmares about teaching. Some of these are classics. Here are a few:

1. You are walking down a corridor on your way to class. There are doors on both sides, and you keep opening doors, but there is always another teacher and another class in each one of the rooms, and no matter how many doors you open, it's never the right door, and you know that you will be late, but your class is nowhere. You wake up in cold sweat.

2. You are about to begin a class, and you know that your lesson plan is completely and carefully set up in your plan book right there in front of you, but when you open the plan book, it is totally empty. All the pages are blank. You cannot remember a single thing. You keep flipping through the pages of the plan book, which is entirely empty. You wake up in cold sweat.

3. Here is a more bizarre one: You are standing in front of the class teaching. You are wearing one of those hospital gowns that tie up in back. You have nothing under it. You know that you are O.K. as long as you just have to face the class, but you also know that you are going to have to turn around to write something on the board. The class knows it too. You see their faces. They are waiting. They know what is about to happen. They are sneering. You wake up in cold sweat.

4. Here is a sinister one: You are lecturing on a topic. Words are coming out of your mouth. You talk but you know that what you are saying is nonsense and that you really don't know what you are talking about. The students in front of you are restless and bored. Some have their feet up, and others are yawning. Then some stand up and walk out. Gradually, as you continue to talk, more students stand up and leave. You keep on talking to fewer and fewer students. Eventually, the whole classroom is empty, but you still keep on talking. Then, finally, you get out and run to your office. Your desk is covered with nasty notes from the students. You wake up in cold sweat.

HAVE AN EMILY MOMENT

In Thornton Wilder's play *Our Town*, Emily, a young mother, dies and finds herself in the town cemetery among other departed town folk. She soon discovers that it is possible to return to one's previous existence or any part of it. One can, she learns, actually re-live one's entire life, provided that one doesn't change anything. Much to her surprise, her new neighbors advise her not to do so.

"Don't do it! Don't do it," they plead.

The stage manager, who in this drama, more or less, performs the role of God, tells her that some have tried such a return, but that they soon enough came back to their cemetery dwelling where "we work on forgetting all that," he explains. The stage manager also lets her know that if she insists on going back; she will not only live her life, but also watch herself living it. "And this," he tells her, "will not be easy."

In spite of all these warnings, Emily decides to return, and since she insists, she is advised to choose a day that had not been special, as any ordinary day would be far more meaningful than she could possibly imagine.

"Choose an unimportant day. Choose the least important day

in your life. It will be important enough," Mrs. Gibbs, who is Emily's mother-in-law, recommends.

Emily had really wanted to re-live her wedding day, but hearing all these warnings, she settles for a return to her twelfth birthday.

We, in the audience, watch her as she re-discovers life, being both Emily, the twelve-year old, and Emily, the returnee, observing. What happens is pain framed by beauty and unbearable sadness.

There is Emily, the outsider, observing the life she has lived, but this time she doesn't just live it. This time, she notices. This time she truly sees. This time she discerns. And we, in the audience, do it with her. Together with Emily, we feel a heightened expansion of all senses and deeper knowledge in the sudden grasp of meaning. The darkened stage grows very bright, giving both the audience and Emily a chance to feel the uncanny shock of lucidity. As the colors expand and swell, Emily, in total clarity, takes it all in. There are the delicious cooking smells of early morning. The kitchen clock ticks. The eggs are frying. The toast burns a bit and all this mingles with the sensation of the sweetness in jam. Emily sees her mother and father as unbearably beautiful. Their voices meld into symphony, and she is encased in a piercing sadness. How could she possibly have lived in this utter beauty and astonishing love without noticing any of it? How can she now endure the awe-inspiring glory of it all? The earthy taste of oatmeal, the sense of yellowness in the wrapping paper, the smell of fried bacon, the curls around her mother's youthful face, the dimple in papa's cheek. All of it suffused in wonder.

Here she is at a perfectly ordinary breakfast scene. She gets a birthday present from Aunt Carrie. It's the postage album she has always wanted, and it has been left on the doorstep together with the morning milk bottles. Emily is admonished by mama to chew the bacon "good and slow" because it will keep her warm on this cold day. Her mother has found something in the attic that has been re-made for Emily. Dad is waiting to hug his birthday girl.

Standing at the edge of the scene is the grown-up, and departed Emily watching it all, and really only comprehending it for the first time. She watches and marvels at how everything unites to produce a perfect sonata, something that her living, twelve-year old self had accepted with simple equanimity of those in the midst of life, those so busy, so very busy with life, where dishes have to be washed and children have to go to school, and milk has to be delivered, and somehow, Emily wants to share the wonder with her mother. She wants to tell her mother about all that had been so mundane—the children who grew up, who went on camping trips, who had accidents. She wants to remind her mother of parenthood and grandparenting, and childbirth. She wants to remind her mama of sorrows. But mostly, she just wants to share her illumination. "Oh, mama, just look at me for one minute as though you really saw me. Mama! Let's look at one another!"

Turning to the stage manager, Emily whispers in wonder, "I didn't notice that all this was going on. Take me back," she begs, "take me back to the dead!"

And as she leaves, she pays homage to the wonder of food and coffee and newly ironed dresses and sleeping and waking up—all those miracles that she had never known about.

I have throughout my life, had those "Emily moments," when I stop to wonder at all of this. The word "Emily" has become my mantra. At moments when I hold life still. When I put it in a frame and allow myself to experience the miracle of it all. At those moments Thornton Wilder's sense of glory surrounds me. This is what great artists can do for us, if we let them. If just for a moment we stop all the business of being busy, all the grief and all the anger to just allow ourselves to experience all of it. To notice. To really see the wonder—the wonder of our lives. Can we still do it? At this stage of our lives, when we have seen it all? When we have done it all? All the preparation? The longing? The fulfillment? The lack of fulfillment? The opportunities we grabbed? The opportunities we missed? And mostly the loves we grasped and held, and cherished?

And recognized? Can we all have an Emily moment each single day? For one moment each day, can we really see life in all that it is and all that it has? For one brief moment, each day can we allow ourselves to recognize it? Can we be aware of how splendidly it has been arranged? Digital clocks, of course, no longer tick; and no one needs to iron those dresses, but there is still food and coffee and at least sometime a good night's sleep and a restful waking. And, yes, there are hot showers, and toothbrushes, and rain on the window panes, and toasted bagels with cream cheese or the sweetness of jam, and good friends, and feet that still walk, and words that can heal, and sometimes there is even a hug. Yes, there is constant misery in the world, yet many of us in the western world live privileged lives, but we still don't really look at one another, and we don't look at the marvel. But we can—for a brief moment each day hear the symphony and sense the miracle of life. For a brief moment, can we observe and notice rather than just live?

Last week, in my poetry class I was idly chatting with two age-mates and we were, as it often happens at this stage in life, recounting our adventures and misadventures and, suddenly we discovered that all three of us had lived in Cambridge, Massachusetts, during the late 50s or early 60s. We looked at one another, and at that moment, there were smiles of happy recognition. For a few minutes, we were in concert, belonging to one another. I counted it as my Emily moment for the day.

So that is what I ask now both of myself and of you, dear reader. Have one Emily moment each day, even if it is very brief. Put the moment in a frame. For just a flash it will be picture perfect —held and noted. It's really our sacred duty to try. Just once a day, let's bask in the gratitude of how wonderful it all is, so very wonderful, even though, of course, clocks do keep ticking, after all.

MY EMILY MOMENT

Rose, my Rose, is about to get off the bus. Somewhere in all her equipment she has discovered a tote. Two bags together with the red handbag have found home in its depth.

Rose moves gingerly down the central isle of the bus. Her walker slants a bit to the side, but it manages the slow, cautious journey to the back door of the bus. A young woman who had just entered the bus two stops earlier reaches out a hand.

"Can I be of help, ma'am?" she inquires softly.

"Yes, sister, you surely can," is the restrained reply.

Somewhere on the journey from West Philly to Center City, Rose has discovered her softer disposition. Those of us who have made the entire journey with her exchange secret smiles. With the help of the cooperative young woman, Rose makes it down the steps. The tote stays firmly planted on her shoulder, and the walker, which now offers both mobility and support suddenly transforms itself from burden to liberator.

Rose straightens up, and lifts her face to the sun. She notices me at the window. She waves and smiles. I wave and smile back.

SOME HISTORIC BACKGROUND

Piotrków Trybunalski, the small Polish town where Natalie was born, is located close to Lodz, the second largest City in Poland. The population of Piotrków today is 80,000. Prior to World War II, about a third of the population was Jewish. The word *Trybunalski* in the town's name means that there was a tribunal (high court) in this Piotrków.

The Treblinka Extermination Camp was assigned only one function and purpose—to kill as many Jews as quickly and efficiently as possible. Operated by the German Nazis, it was located in a forest northeast of Warsaw. Seven to nine hundred thousand Jews were murdered there. The victims were killed by suffocation through carbon monoxide. Natalie's parents died at Treblinka.

Huta Kara and Huta Hortensia were both factories that produced decorative glass objects. During the war they evidently helped to build parts of weapons for the Nazi cause, and were able to use Jewish slave labor. Natalie spent close to a year at Huta Kara. She does remember the cold winter. She recalls that winter because Kuba, Helena's husband, made a sled for her.

Vogel was the overseer at Huta Kara but Christman owned the factory. During her one and only post-war journey to Piotrków, Natalie learned that Christman had escaped to Argentina after the war.

Ravensbrück Concentration Camp took women from all over Europe. Mostly they were Jews, whose demise was planned through systematic starvation, but there were also Gypsies, as well as German law-breakers, especially prostitutes. There were also children in the camp, and 140 women were sterilized. There was a crematorium, and medical experiments were performed.

Siemens, close to the camp, used slave labor provided by the camp.

PHOTOS

*Natalie's father Adek Chojnacki about age 45. He was
murdered at Treblinka around 1940*

Natalie's mother Regina about age 40. She was murdered at Treblinka around 1940

Natalie and Helena in Sweden (1947)

Sixteen-year-old Natalie in Sweden just before she went to the US

Natalie in the kitchen of the old house in Talpiot, Jerusalem

Natalie and her husband John in Israel around 2010

*A happy family Hess. From left to right: Debby, Natalie,
John, Rebecka, and Tamar*

*Railroad track that Natalie took from Pjotrkow to
Ravensbruck (2016)*

*Natalie and granddaughter Rachel in front of her
grandmother's store and house on 6 Farna street in Pjotrkow
(2016)*

*Natalie, her daughters Tamar and Debby and granddaughter
Rachel in front of old synagogue in Pjotrkow which is now
converted to a library (2016)*

Natalie in front of a synagogue wall with bullet holes where Jews were shot to death while praying in Pjotrkow (2016)

Natalie in Jewish cemetery at Pjotrkow pointing to tombstone erected for her family after WW2 (2016)

Natalie's 80's birthday in her Philadelphia apartment.
Natalie accompanied by her daughters. Top row: Debby and
Tammy; bottom row: Natalie and Becky

ABOUT THE AUTHOR

Natalie Hess (Natalia Chojnacka) was born in Piotrków Trybunalski, Poland in 1936. She was five years old when her parents perished at Treblinka, a Nazi extermination camp.

Through a series of fortunate events, she was able to survive ghettoes, and the Ravensbrück concentration camp to be saved in 1945 by the Swedish Red Cross.

She had spent seven years in Sweden, when she received a visa that would allow her at age sixteen, to join relatives in Evansville, Indiana.

Natalie earned a Master's Degree from Harvard and a Ph.D. from the University of Arizona. She has lived and worked both in the US and in Israel and has served as a teacher educator in six countries.

QUESTIONS FOR DISCUSSION

1. In B'reshit—In the Beginning or She is Me, the author says that she does not want to live a "life endlessly propelled by its unfairness and imperfections." What does she mean by this? Do you agree with her? Why or why not?

2. In Part I, Holocaust Spider Webs in My Head, why is it so important for Natalie to make sure she tells the young German couple about the synagogue?

3. What do you think about Natalie's early family life in Part I, Holocaust, How I Learned to be a Lady?

4. How does "being a Jew is dangerous" affect Natalie and the Gentile family who is hiding her in Part I, Holocaust, Keeping a Child and Into the Ghetto?

5. There is plenty to cry about for everyone involved in Part I, Holocaust, Into the Ghetto but the little girl decides not to cry. In your opinion, who should cry? Why?

6. What happens between the child and Helena in Part I, Holocaust, *Registered*? Why is this significant?

7. Occasionally in life things happen that appear to be "miracles" or just strangely coincidental. Such is the incident in Part 1, Holocaust, *The Boy Who Needed a Playmate*. Have you had such incidents in your life, and how have you defined them?

8. Why does the child feel guilty in Part 1 Holocaust, *Jacket Exchange, Train Ride, and Arrival*? Is the guilt justified? Why or why not?

9. Can you understand the author when, in Part 1, Holocaust, *Lice* she tells us that her girlhood had been stolen?

10. The text offers several examples of how children speak very casually about death. Do you have any thoughts about such talk?

11. In Part I Holocaust, *So, What Is It All About* the author returns to Poland. What do you find most significant during the visit? Please explain your choice.

12. Which of the author's experiences in various school settings compare with your own?

13. Do the author's observations of life in the United States during the late 50s ring true? Do any of these observations parallel your own or the experiences of anyone close to you?

14. In Part IV, Life in Israel, *Ali and his Israeli Teacher* Ali calls his "nice American" teacher "naive." Do you agree? Why or why not?

15. Why might Ali need a secret identity in Part IV, Life in Israel, *Ali and his Israeli Teacher*?

16. In Part II, Life in Sweden, *Leaving*, Natalie tells us that she feels trapped in a "bubble of aloneness." Can you recognize this feeling? What could a sympathetic grownup tell Natalie to make her feel better.

17. In Part II, Life in Sweden, *Two Weeks at Sea*, why does Natalie feel insulted by the Statue of Liberty? Do you think that the feeling is justified?

18. In Part III, Newcomer in America, *AMBJ* Natalie feels that she exists in "a bubble of contentment." Compare this bubble with the one in question 16. What has happened? Are these feelings justified?

19. In Part III, Newcomer in America, *AMBJ* it is said "You just get yourself a husband. That's what you do in college. That's the main thing. Once you have a husband, everything else will fall into place." Please comment.

20. In Part III, Newcomer in America, *The Hess Dress* the author states "Clearly the stain exposes my vulnerability." Please comment.

NOTES

Spider Webs in my Head

1. Ravensbrück was a women's concentration camp located in Northern Germany, 90 kilometers north of Berlin.

Keeping a Child

1. Almost immediately, after the Germans occupied Poland, they instituted a long list of laws regarding Jews. Jews in the General Government had to wear a white armband with the Star of David in blue on it, while those in the annexed Polish territories (including Piotrków Trybunalski) were ordered to display the yellow star on all outer garments. Jewish children were not allowed to attend school. Jewish professionals lost their jobs. Jews were allowed to live only in certain designated neighborhoods. These neighborhoods became the large ghetto. But as more and more Jews were deported to concentration camps, the ghetto grew smaller and eventually became known as the small ghettos.

Registered

1. Jewish councils, made up of former community leaders, who saved their own lives by delivering Jews directly to the trains that were headed for the death camps. They were usually the last ones slated for death.

Lice

1. There were four of us on each shelf-bed. Helena and I shared the shelf with a mother and her daughter. Helena and the mother faced each other, and I faced the daughter. For many years after the war, whenever I visited Helena, she would bring up the subject of this sleeping arrangement and grumbled, "Why did you sleep facing the daughter while I faced the mother? We could have had more room the other way around." Note: these shelves were like a crowded eight-story bunk bed.

Holding Time

1. Mezuzah is of biblical origin and therefore carries great weight. "And you shall inscribe them on the doorposts (*mezuzot*) (plural of mezuzah) of our house and on your gates" (Deuteronomy 6:9, 11:20). What is to be inscribed? Divine instruction is very clear: "The words that I shall tell you this day": that you shall love your God, believe only in Him, keep His commandments, and pass all of this on to your children. https://www.myjewishlearning.com/article/mezuzah/ A Jewish home feels right once the mezuzah (a parchment with the blessing safely housed in a case) is mounted on the front door frame.

Sweden, The National Anthems of My Life

1. Folke Bernadotte (1896-1948) was a Swedish diplomat and nobleman noted for his negotiation for the release of 31,000 prisoners from German concentration camps.
2. In the *Book of Esther*, Esther the Jewish harem girl turned queen saves her people from slaughter, by cleverly manipulating her new husband into nullifying his own previous edict for genocide that had been dictated by his evil adviser Haman. Jewish tradition celebrates the rescue in the spring holiday of Purim.
3. From the poem, "The Death of the Hired man".

Of Cows and Cowards

1. "I don't know anything. I don't understand anything," in Swedish.

The Six-Day War

1. "Dodah" is the Hebrew word for "aunt" "Aunt' is frequently used as an honorific by children to any older female. Dodah Marta, the local nursery school teacher, is addressed in this way both by her young charges and by their parents. She is in charge of my children during the day.
2. Sunday (first day) is the first day of the work-week in Israel.
3. Aliyah—Hebrew for "rising up." A commonly used term for immigration from the Diaspora to Israel.
4. Irish born and British-educated Chaim (Vivian) Herzog, who later became president of Israel, provided constant war analysis throughout the war the Six-Day War. His soothing and well-stated messages gave those of us who sat in shelters much needed support.

The Balabusta

1. Yiddish is a Germanic language spoken by Jews throughout the Germanic and Slavic worlds. It is a Creole composed mostly of medieval German sprinkled with Polish and Hebrew. It is written in Hebrew characters.

Ali and his Israeli Teacher

1. The First Intifada (also known as simply the "intifada" or intifadah was a Palestinian uprising against the Israeli occupation of the Palestinian Territories, which lasted from December 1987 to 1993.

Morning Walks in Mevaseret Zion

1. Arabic for prostitute
2. "Good morning" in Arabic
3. "Good morning" in Hebrew
4. "Morning light" standard answer in the morning greeting formula

The Improbable Richard

1. The holiest day in the Jewish calendar. It is the one day during, the temple period, the year when the high priest, dressed in white, would enter the holy of holiest to declare Judaism's seminal prayer. The day is observed with fast and prayer.
2. Didion, J. (2005). *The Year of Magical Thinking*. New York: Vintage International.

Made in the USA
Middletown, DE
19 October 2020